WORDS IN MOTION

An Interactive Approach to Writing

TEACHER'S GUIDE

David Olsher

Talbot F. Hamlin

Oxford University Press

Oxford University Press
198 Madison Avenue
New York, NY 10016 USA

Walton Street
Oxford OX2 6DP England

OXFORD is a trademark of Oxford University Press.

ISBN 0-19-434459-2

Editorial Manager: Chris Foley
Developmental Editor: Bev Curran
Project Manager: Talbot F. Hamlin
Production Editor: Sharon Kaufman
Production Manager: Abram Hall

Text design by PC&F, Inc.
Illustrations by Doug Buchman
Cover design by Susan Brorein
Cover illustration by Michael McGurl

Printing (last digit):   10   9   8   7   6   5   4   3   2   1

Printed in the United States of America.

Contents

Teaching *Words in Motion*—Unit By Unit

Teaching *Words in Motion*—Part 4: Project Writing

Words in Motion Answer Key

About
Words in Motion

Words in Motion was created with the basic philosophy that writing is a process aimed at real communication with other people. Although many parts of the writing process involve individual creative and problem-solving work, many other parts of writing involve communication, collaboration, and consultation with others. This book seeks a balance between these two sides of writing.

Words in Motion also seeks a healthy balance between developing writing-process skills and cultivating an awareness of the characteristics of different kinds of genres or writing products. Learners are encouraged to experiment, explore, and craft their writing to fit its intended purpose and audience. Further, the writing topics in *Words in Motion* have been selected to interest students and to give them an opportunity to write about themselves and their own interests as well as to write personal and business letters, résumés, and job applications.

The activities in *Words in Motion* are designed to introduce and review many useful writing practices and to exploit the communicative and social environment of the classroom. Students can work together at times, and alone at others. They can write for each other or for readers outside of the class. Throughout the lesson sequence, students are guided toward awareness of their intended readers, the purpose of the written product, and the genre or text type that fits this audience and purpose. Writing checklists, clear guidance, and lots of examples help to make the process both enjoyable and manageable and to create more confident and independent writers.

Grammar, which is always an issue in ESL/EFL writing, is a highly individualized subject for learners as well as teachers. It is assumed that students using *Words in Motion* have practiced sentence-level grammar, including basic punctuation, use of verb tenses, subject-verb agreement, basic use of prepositions, and pronoun agreement. It is also assumed that students in a given class will have different levels of English language skills. To accommodate the range of needs and expectations, minimal grammar review exercises are integrated into the units. These exercises refer learners and teachers to lessons in the Grammar Clinic section at the end of the Student Book. These Grammar Clinic lessons can be used for self-study, as classroom lessons, or as individualized homework assignments. Clear models of a variety of different types of writing are provided in the Writing Samples section of the Student Book.

The *Words in Motion* Student Book

Words in Motion is divided into six sections:

> Part 1: Writing about Yourself (Units 1-5)
>
> Part 2: Writing Letters (Units 6-10)
>
> Part 3: Ideas, Opinions, and Paragraphs (Units 11 and 12)
>
> Part 4: Project Writing
>
> Writing Samples
>
> Grammar Clinic

Parts 1 and 2 of the book include writing projects as a way to consolidate and review what was learned. Part 3 provides an introduction to writing of two very different types of material with which most students are familiar—tourist guides and movie reviews. Part 4, with a choice of five writing projects and guidance for project planning and tracking, presents rich opportunities for learners to work more independently and pursue their own interests and goals while still following clear steps.

Writing projects not only provide memorable writing experiences for learners, but also allow them to consolidate and further master the writing skills that were introduced and reviewed in previous units of the Student Book.

TIMING AND STRUCTURE OF THE UNITS

Each of the uniformly structured five-page units in Parts 1, 2, and 3 is designed to be covered in a 60- to 90-minute class period. Lesson pacing will vary, depending on the level of the students and the number of expansion activities, such as Grammar Clinic lessons, done in class. The four activity pages in each unit—Warm Ups, Writing Matters, Page for Practice, and Put It in Writing—present a sequence of activities to engage the learner, present a clearly focused writing point, and lead to a productive pre-writing or writing activity. In many units, the writing activity may usefully be completed as homework, especially when some students take longer to write than others.

FLEXIBILITY

While the exercises are targeted for lower-intermediate level students, the open-ended nature of the writing activities makes *Words in Motion* useful for higher-level students as well. The length and quality of the completed writings will vary with the level of student, but the writing types and topics should prove interesting and useful for a wide range of students. This flexibility makes the book useful for mixed-level writing classes. The Writing Samples and the Grammar Clinic lessons should appeal to intermediate and even upper-intermediate students as well as to lower-intermediate learners.

LEARNING LOGS AND PROJECT PLANNING FORMS

Short, simple Learning Logs at the ends of Parts 1 and 2 of the Student Book (pages 26 and 55) ask learners to look back at the activities completed and reflect on what they enjoyed learning and where they need help. (These Learning Logs are also provided as reproducible masters at the end of this Teacher's Guide.) Part 4 begins with a Project and Goals page (Student Book page 72), which guides learners through an analysis of possible projects and helps to establish personal learning goals before the students choose a project. The Project Log (page 73) allows students to track their progress and record their reactions to their project work, and the Project Planning Form (page 74) helps learners think about the audience, purpose, register, and pre-writing strategies before starting projects. A General Learning Log for use with students' project work is also included with the reproducible materials at the end of this Teacher's Guide.

WRITING PROJECTS

Parts 1 and 2 of the Student Book end with writing projects designed to allow learners to consolidate and extend the writing and language skills developed in the units. Part 1 ends with a single writing project: a personal profile. Part 2 ends with a choice of two writing projects: a pen pal letter or an information letter. Part 3 introduces writing movie reviews and tourist pamphlets; both projects are included in expanded form in Part 4.

Part 4 combines project planning activities with five writing projects for learners to choose from. An easy-to-follow Writing Project page, which includes the format for the particular writing type and a list of steps to complete the project, and a Project Skills page, with project tips and language tips to help make the project interesting and successful, are provided for each of the writing projects. By varying the number and length of the projects, you can fit *Words in Motion* to the level and time constraints of your individual classes.

WRITING SAMPLES

Suitable models for writing are very important and may not always be readily available. Accordingly, the Writing Samples section of the Student Book provides such models as an extra learning resource for all of the writing projects in Parts 1 through 4.

GRAMMAR CLINIC

The Grammar Clinic section provides a set of twelve independent two-page grammar review lessons, which can be used in a variety of ways. The first page of each lesson reviews the rules for and presents examples of an element of grammar. The second page provides structured drills, which are usually followed by open-ended practice. References to some of these lessons appear in Units 1, 4, 8, 10, and 12. This additional practice is suitable for either self-study or in-class grammar reinforcement. The Grammar Clinic lessons can also be selected as needed for a whole class and done as homework or as in-class get-started activities. You may want to recommend specific Grammar Clinic lessons to particular students or let individual learners choose lessons for themselves. While by no means exhaustive, these lessons provide an excellent review of basic grammar points for lower-level students.

Additional Learning Resources

To handle corrections and help students build awareness of their own mistakes, this Teacher's Guide contains a number of reproducible masters, including a chart of editing correction symbols (which also appears on the inside back cover of the Student Book), a Mistake Log to help students keep track of repeated mistakes so they can focus on self-correction, a Writer's Checklist to be used with any writing that is being turned in after revision, the Learning Logs from Parts 1 and 2, a General Learning Log, and a set of Vocabulary Study Tools.

It is a good idea to have the students create their own notebooks in which to keep the reproducible resources and drafts, notes, and writing samples that are not found in the Student Book . This includes all project work, the completed project planning forms, and any optional vocabulary pages. The notebook itself becomes a resource and a portfolio of all work completed. It allows students to see, in a tangible way, their progress and the body of work they have completed.

Classroom Management and Logistics

DOING WRITTEN WORK

The *Words in Motion* Student Book is intended to be consumable. The majority of exercises are answered by writing in the book. In some instances, however, such as the Writing Projects and certain Put It in Writing activities, students are expected to complete an exercise on their own paper, not in the book. In any instance in which a student finds the space in the book insufficient for her or his response, that student should be encouraged to continue the response on a separate piece of paper. (Be sure, however, that the student understands the instructions and is not doing more writing than is necessary.) This material would then go into the student notebook discussed above.

PAIR AND GROUP WORK

Some activities specify pair or group work. It is a good idea to get students into a regular routine for finding partners and for forming pairs or groups so that groupings and regroupings can be accomplished easily when needed. This may need to be worked on at the start of the term for some classes. Make sure that students understand that pair and group work is often helpful for writing, problem solving, and language learning. For activities that do not specify pairs or groups, you may want to let students (1) work individually, (2) work individually but then meet with partners to compare answers, or (3) work in pairs, then share answers in small groups, and possibly report their findings to the class.

TRADING STUDENT BOOKS OR PAPERS

In some activities, students are asked to trade books and write their comments directly in their partner's

book. In other activities, learners are directed to trade first drafts and write their comments directly on the draft. In each case, clear instructions are provided in the Student Book and in this Guide.

LEARNER CHOICE

Because learner choice increases motivation and encourages greater autonomy, students are given increasing choice in their writing topics as the book progresses. The writing projects especially lend themselves to learner choice. Learners not only select the focus and the content of each project, but they also get to choose which project to complete in Part 2 and have even greater choice in Part 4. You may also wish to let students decide whether to work on projects individually, in pairs, or in small groups. An additional place you can introduce learner choice is in the selection of Grammar Clinic lessons.

ASSESSMENT AND GRADING

In order to cultivate the freedom of the writing process, it is a good idea to assign simple check (✓), check-plus (✓+), or check-minus (✓–) grades for pre-writing, drafts, Grammar Clinic lessons, and other homework. Letter grades can be reserved for completed second drafts and projects. This serves to complement a process of experimentation and development working toward a completed product. When correcting grammar mistakes, it is most meaningful to the student to mark only those elements that have already been explicitly covered in class, so that a manageable list of grammar elements is developed gradually over the course of the school term.

GOING BEYOND THE STUDENT BOOK

It is important that your students be exposed to as many actual examples of English-language writing as possible. These samples should be of similar kinds or genres to those in the Student Book, but they should be of more specific interest to your class. Ideally, these samples should be found by your students and brought to class, but you may need to supplement them and you will probably want to suggest particular source material. You may want to create a class writing file for use as a resource during project work. Have the students look for useful vocabulary in these texts, consider their purposes, and think about their intended audiences. Also ask students what they find most interesting about them.

Another useful way to go beyond the Student Book is to let your class create a magazine or booklet using their best writing projects. Such a class magazine can be a very rewarding and motivating project to end the school year.

Using this Teacher's Guide

STRUCTURE OF THIS GUIDE

▶ "Teaching *Words in Motion*—Strands and Strategies," with expanded discussions of particular strands and activity types and suggestions for making corrections and for assessment and grading; "Teaching *Words in Motion*—Unit by Unit," with Teaching Notes for each exercise and project; and "Teaching *Words in Motion*—Part 4: Project Writing," with discussions of the projects in Part 4.

▶ Answer keys for all the unit exercises that have "correct" answers and for all the Grammar Clinic exercises. These can be photocopied and distributed to the students for self-correction if desired.

▶ Reproducible resources, including a chart of correction symbols, a Mistake Log, a Writer's Checklist, several Learning Logs, and Vocabulary Study Tools.

PLANNING

You will probably want to use the teaching notes and reproducible resources to plan your lessons, and note special activities or considerations for particular lessons, such as homework due and activities that may need to be completed at home or at the next class meeting. You can also note which Writing Samples or Grammar Clinic lessons go with particular units and consider possible extensions of the material in the Student Book.

WHILE YOU TEACH

The simple, clear teaching notes for each unit provide the crucial information you will need. The answer key can be referred to in the classroom as you teach each lesson or appropriate sections can be photocopied for easy reference by you or the students.

REPRODUCIBLE MATERIALS

Take advantage of the reproducible materials that are provided in this Guide to enhance your use of the Student Book. You may also wish to reproduce answers to some of the unit lessons and the Grammar Clinic lessons to expedite self-correction or partner-correction for these lessons in class. (You will probably wish to collect these copied answers after the students have corrected their exercises so that you can use them with future classes.)

Teaching *Words in Motion*— Strands and Strategies

Strands and Strategies: An Overview

This section, which is the core of this Teacher's Guide, goes hand in hand with the two sections that follow it, "Teaching *Words in Motion*—Unit by Unit" and "Teaching *Words in Motion*—Part 4: Project Writing." Its purpose is to provide an orientation to the basic strands that run throughout *Words in Motion* and to suggest some strategies for implementing these in teaching the different kinds of exercises in the book. You will probably want to read this section carefully before you begin teaching *Words in Motion* and return to it periodically as particular kinds of exercises and activities are introduced.

The Language of Communication

Insofar as possible, English should be the language of your classroom. Encourage students to speak and to write in English when they are in class. This includes both their communication with you and with classmates. Class business should be conducted in English as much as possible. This consistent use of English provides valuable practice for language learners and helps to build the students' confidence in their ability to accomplish the practical tasks involved in the study of writing in English. If students ask or answer questions in their own language, simply say, "Could you say that in English, please?" However, if you speak your students' language, it may occasionally be helpful to use that language to explain a grammatical rule, a complex point, or a vocabulary item. Occasionally, some pre-writing activities or project planning may be done in the native language as well, if this promotes more successful writing

and is limited in time. Such practical use of the students' native language when necessary can be a useful exception to the general rule of using English for classroom communication. (Obviously, this is not very practical if the class has students with a variety of native languages.)

The Writing Process

Parts 1, 2, and 3 of *Words in Motion* each take students through one complete cycle of the writing process. This process is basic to the "healthy balance" of process and product referred to at the beginning of this Guide. The writing process as used here includes the following eight steps:

1. Orientation. *Think about the goals, the type of writing, and the topic.* Be sure students understand they are getting ready for a new topic as they begin the process in Unit 1 and again in Unit 6.

2. Pre-writing. *Gather and generate ideas and information, then organize them.* Pre-writing may include making lists, interviewing, taking notes, reading, Quick Writes (which involve writing quickly with a focus only on ideas, not on form, grammar, or spelling), and using idea bubbles (introduced in Part 3 of the Student Book). The emphasis is on gathering ideas to be selected and organized later. By the end of Part 3, students should have developed a repertoire of pre-writing techniques that will enable them to select the tools that will be most useful when they encounter new writing tasks.

3. Drafting. *Put ideas down in sentences in rough draft form, keeping the intended audience in mind.* Let

students know that most successful writers write several drafts before producing a finished piece of writing. In drafting, the focus is not on perfect spelling or grammar but on content, ideas, the intended reader, and the general form. Knowing that one is writing a draft that one will have the opportunity to revise later takes away the pressure of feeling that everything must be perfect and allows for more creativity.

4. Peer editing. *Trade drafts and read and comment on your partner's draft.* Focusing on content and overall form, students write questions and comments telling their partner what they feel needs to be added or clarified from a reader's point of view. Peer editing not only helps the partner, it also helps the editor to become a better reader and editor of his or her own work. Emphasize that peer editing is *not* correcting—it is responding to the content and cooperating with the writer to help her or him improve the writing. Tell students not to correct grammar. Encourage positive comments rather than negative ones. Explain that careful reading and thinking are necessary if one is to make specific comments and questions that will be truly helpful to the writer. Tell students not to skip or ignore parts of the writing that they find confusing, but instead to make a note or write a question so the writer can clarify or explain better in the second draft. (Students may be interested to know that nearly all the writing they see published has been read and commented on by several people in just this way before it reached its final form.)

5. Revision. *Mark changes, additions, and corrections on your own drafts to prepare for rewriting.* Part 1 of the book focuses on revising for content. Part 2 introduces self-editing for grammatical form, punctuation, and paragraphing. Grammar is an important focus of self-editing in *Words in Motion.* Several of the Warm Ups exercises and other activities help to develop self-editing skills. It is a good policy to announce in advance the grammar points on which you will be grading so that students can keep this in mind as they begin the process of self-editing and revision.

6. Rewriting. *Write a second draft , incorporating all revision markings, added content, and any new ideas that arise as you write.* Let students know that this is, in part, a mechanical process of following revision notes, but that it also can be creative, since new ideas often come up while writing a second draft.

7. Proofreading. *Read the second draft looking for—and correcting—mistakes in spelling, punctuation, format, and any remaining grammatical errors.* The basic approach is for students to look for items that have been explicitly taught in class, so the list of items to

correct for will expand as the course progresses. It will include those items covered in the 12 units plus any additional items covered by the full class in the Grammar Clinic lessons.

8. Follow-up. *Trade drafts in pairs or in small groups.* This follow-up avoids the syndrome in which writing is looked at as only done for the teacher and for a grade. Sometimes referred to as "publication," this last step in the writing process provides a sense that the writing really is for communication—which is, after all, the real goal of most writing, and the primary goal of *Words in Motion.*

Quick Writes

Some students may "freeze up" when first asked to complete a Quick Write, especially if they have been conditioned to feel they have to get every detail of every sentence correct before they write or speak. Instead, in their Quick Writes they are permitted, and even urged, to write without worrying about grammar, spelling, or form. The following suggestions may help to "thaw" these students' writer's block.

1. Let your students know that Quick Writes are a valuable, perfectly respectable, and fun tool used by many successful professional writers for brainstorming and generating ideas.

2. Ask if students ever write quick informal notes or memos in their own language, or if any of them keep journals or diaries just for themselves. Explain that a Quick Write is a little like each of these kinds of writing. Emphasize that students will never be graded or judged on the grammar or spelling in a Quick Write. It's simply a fast way to get their ideas on record, and all that matters are the ideas and making a sincere effort.

3. Let students know that they should generally aim to write in sentences, but shouldn't worry if some of these are incomplete or incorrectly formed.

4. Let students know that if they can't think of the right word or phrase to express an idea, they can just write a blank line to hold the place of the missing word or phrase and go on writing.

5. Emphasize that a Quick Write should be fun!

6. Finally, never comment on or correct students' grammar or spelling in a Quick Write. And don't be surprised if some students' Quick Writes are longer or shorter than others. Respond only to the content.

Once students are accustomed to doing Quick Writes, you may want to use them as occasional warm-up exercises. Just put two or three questions on the board, ask students to pick one question, and give them ten minutes to write.

Pair and Group Work

As discussed earlier, pair and group work is central to the teaching of writing in *Words in Motion.* The instructions in the Student Book specify pair or group work at certain times, but you should feel free to introduce additional pair or group work to the activities as you see fit; working in pairs offers security to many students and helps build confidence. Here are some things to consider when working with pairs and groups.

1. Encourage students to communicate in English even with those who share the same native language. (See the discussion of "The Language of Communication" above.)

2. Vary the composition of pairs and groups with each new piece of writing to be done. In general, this will mean, except when activity instructions specify working with a new partner, that partners or group members will be the same throughout a unit or while working on a particular project, but they will change for the next unit or project. Ideally, each student should have the opportunity to work at some time during the school term with every other student, although this may be impractical in large classes.

3. If you have an odd number of students in your class, make one pair a trio, but be sure that the same student does not always have to work with two partners rather than with one.

4. Early in the school year, establish and rehearse set routines for pair and group work so that when you give cues such as "work with a partner," "find a new partner," or "form groups," students will understand and respond promptly.

5. If you want pairs or groups to work together, give them very specific tasks, just as is done in the Student Book. Even if you just want students to read the instructions and let you know if they have any questions, you can make the task specific by asking each pair to think of one or two questions about things that are unclear or confusing. Then you can call on the pairs to report their questions to the class.

6. Call on pairs or groups to report their findings, whether these are questions, answers, vocabulary items, or information about each other. Be sure to let the pairs or groups know in advance what kind of reporting you will expect, for example, "I'm going to call on you to put your answers on the board in five minutes." To be most effective, don't tell the pairs or groups who you will call on, so that everyone will be prepared to answer all questions. This is a gentle way of putting some pressure on all groups to have the answers required. Correct the answers together. Ask the class if the responses a pair or group gives are correct. If they are not, ask the class for help in correcting them.

7. Progress from small groups to larger ones. Pairs may answer some questions, then check the answers in larger groups, and finally report to the entire class. Similarly, group work may be followed by groups reporting to each other and then to the whole class.

8. Be there to help. Answer questions, clarify instructions, but do not do the students' work for them. You may want to circulate as pairs and groups work, to emphasize your availability, to check that pairs and groups are on task, to encourage them to speak in English, and so on.

Learning Logs

Learning Logs help students to reflect on what they are doing and to build awareness of their progress. In this way, the logs help learners to take more active control of their own learning.

Two Learning Logs are found in *Words in Motion,* one at the end of Unit 5 (Student Book page 26) and one at the end of Unit 10 (page 55). Both are also provided in the Reproducible Resources section of this Teacher's Guide. These Learning Logs help learners take stock of their progress before they recycle the skills practiced in a writing project. A General Learning Log, also in the Reproducible Resources section, can be used with Part 3 and the writing projects in Part 4. The basic process for completing all three Learning Logs is the same, although those for Parts 1 and 2 are simpler than the General Log, which is intended to be used later.

In using the Learning Logs, students first review the work they have completed. They then answer questions about what they enjoyed, what made them feel successful, and what areas they feel they need more practice with. Finally, they note vocabulary or other language skills they feel will be useful for them to remember.

To administer a Learning Log, make sure students have their Student Books, research, pre-writing, and drafts with them. Let them know that the Learning Log is important and will help them to remember and be able to use what they have learned. Then give students a copy of the Learning Log, or have them turn to the appropriate page in the Student Book. Ask students to look back over their work and the various exercises they completed, such as Grammar Clinic lessons, unit exercises, and Project Skills pages, and think about what they learned. Then, and only then, have them answer the questions about their work. Have students note vocabulary or, for the General Learning Log, other language skills they want to remember. Collect the Learning Logs, but let the students know that they will be graded only on their effort, not on the content or grammar of their answers. Also tell them that the information on their Learning Logs can help you provide a better class for them.

Writing Projects

Writing projects allow students to recycle and apply the kinds of language and writing skills they have learned in the units of the book. Projects also give students a chance to make more choices about the focus and topic of their writing and to work more independently.

Words in Motion is structured to build gradually from a sequence of teacher-directed individual, pair, and small-group activities toward more independent project-oriented work for which you often act in the role of a resource for students working on their own writing projects. Part 1 ends with a single project, the Personal Profile, which gives students experience in applying the vocabulary, language skills, and writing process skills already practiced to a project focused on a person outside the class. Part 2 culminates with a choice of two projects, a pen pal letter and an information letter. The choice allows students to pursue their own interests and opens up the writing classroom to more than one project going on at the same time. Part 3 prepares students to try other kinds of writing, such as tourist pamphlets and movie reviews, and Part 4 provides a choice of additional projects. Depending on time, resources, and teacher and student preferences, it is possible to have pairs and individual students working on a variety of projects at the same time. This can help to build the confidence and autonomy of developing writers, but at the same time it poses problems of planning and management.

ADVANCE PLANNING

To manage writing projects in the classroom, it is important to consider the following:

1. *Choices.* Decide in advance what choices you want to allow students to make. You may want to open the choices completely for issues of pair versus individual work, which and/or how many projects to do, or the specific content of projects—or you may want to provide some guidance and set limits. For example, you may want to limit the subjects of the personal profile to people who are older than the students or to people who are native speakers of English. Some limits may help students to have more successful projects; on the other hand, too many limits may reduce the students' chance to invest themselves in project work.

2. *Deadlines.* Deadlines for the various phases of a project can help to motivate students and keep them on target, but they should be flexible enough to allow for extension if necessary, since you cannot always predict how much time a project will require. Again, too much rigidity can erode students' interest in project work, so a balance needs to be reached.

3. *Standards and requirements.* Set these to fit the level of your students. Rough guidelines for the length and the quality of the finished project should be discussed at the outset and agreed upon. Be flexible, but be sure to set some standards and be sure the students understand that you expect them to follow these.

4. *Product format.* Discuss what form the finished product will take, including such issues as typing (including use of word processors or computers) versus handwriting; layout; and graphics. While content and writing process are the main focus, realistic and practical product specifications should be discussed in advance so that neither the student nor the teacher is caught by surprise.

5. *Follow-up.* This is the final step of the writing process, and should not be bypassed. Suggestions for follow-up include oral presentations of personal profiles, stories, or speeches to the entire class or to other classes, making a class booklet or magazine of the class's projects, bulletin board or hallway displays of completed projects, and a chart keeping track of letters sent and responses received.

STAGES OF A WRITING PROJECT

All writing projects go through the same stages. It is important to make sure that none of these stages is omitted in the interest of time.

1. *Orientation to topic.* In Parts 1, 2, and 3, this is thoroughly covered in the units preceding the projects. In Part 4, most of the project topics should be fairly familiar to most students, but some topics may be unfamiliar, for example, applying for a job.

2. *Orientation to the type of writing and its goals.* For Parts 1, 2, and 3, this has been done in the units. In Part 4, it is focused and clarified in the project steps, which involve reading a sample in the Writing Samples section and looking at a simplified generic format for the particular type of writing. More examples of the different writing types or genres—found and brought into the classroom—are also useful to show the students how real-world résumés, business letters, movie reviews, and tourist pamphlets look.

3. *Using language skills and task skills.* Specific language and task skills need to be used to complete the projects, and specific project skills exercises are provided for support in these areas. Be sure to preview the Project Skills pages in advance so that you can help students to implement their projects in

your own school and community with the resources available.

4. *Pre-writing and data collection.* This takes various forms depending on the nature of the writing project. It may involve idea generation or research and can include planning and conducting interviews, visiting libraries or embassies, collecting pamphlets or maps, taking notes, listing, and a variety of other activities. The project steps and project skills activities provide some guidance, but be sure to check with students to help them solve any problems and make the best use of resources in your school and community.

5. *Writing a first draft.* Notes, ideas, and information are gathered, organized, and used to write a first draft. Remind students that this stage of the writing process is mainly concerned with making sense of the ideas and presenting the information in a particular writing form. Encourage students to keep a target audience in mind—which could be foreign tourists, students and teachers in the school, a business, or a government agency. Accuracy of grammar is not the main focus and can be improved later.

6. *Getting feedback.* Peer editing is an important part of the development of writing skills as well as the improvement of the draft, so encourage students to do their best at giving peer comments. Scheduling and deadlines are important so that groups or individuals can trade drafts and provide responses—so set peer-editing dates in advance. Drafts and peer-editing comments should be saved together in the students' notebooks, and you should check to see that a serious effort was made by the peer editors. Peer editing should be done with the intended purpose and audience in mind, so writers should note this information on the drafts. For letters that are to be sent out, such as job applications and information requests, it is a good idea for you to give feedback to the students as well.

7. *Revision and second draft.* Remind students that they can use revision markings, more pre-writing, and notes on other paper as preparation for writing the second draft. Encourage revisions that will make their projects more complete, better organized, and more successful (for example, a scarier story, a more effective résumé, or a more informative tourist pamphlet).

8. *Follow-up.* See the discussion under "Advance Planning" above.

CLASSROOM MANAGEMENT FOR WRITING PROJECTS

You will probably want to devote two or more class sessions to project work for each project. This may involve all students working independently, all students working in pairs, or a mix of independent and pair work. (Note that projects produced by pairs should generally be more substantial than individual projects, but students' level and motivation will also affect the results.) In this workshop-style classroom, you will be serving mainly as a consultant and resource person, going from student to student as needed. However, it is still useful to maintain some of the organization of the classroom. You can start the class with a group activity, such as a Grammar Clinic lesson; vocabulary work in which individuals contribute to a list of useful vocabulary displayed on the board; project skills, such as editing a sample draft; or discussions of project problems and solutions, which can be shared with the class. After a short whole-class activity, announce that you will break up for project work until the last few minutes of the class. Close the project work toward the end of the class and finish with a short activity, such as a vocabulary guessing game, the reading aloud of an interesting project in progress, or the sharing of a solution to a problem, such as how to lay out a pamphlet or where to find information. Also review the ongoing schedule, with due dates and other class information, at these closing and opening activities.

Vocabulary Study Tools

Many language learners feel that vocabulary is one of the aspects of language that they need the most help with. This book encourages the learning of vocabulary in context through the many samples of writing and through exercises that include vocabulary relevant to the topic and type of writing. A good way to reinforce and complement this approach to learning is by collecting and grouping vocabulary in various ways. The simple vocabulary boxes in the Learning Logs that appear at the end of Parts 1 and 2 in the Student Book (pages 26 and 55) provide a basic list, but the reproducible Vocabulary Study Tools that appear at the end of this Guide give the student additional options.

WHEN TO DO VOCABULARY WORK

Working on vocabulary before students write a draft gives them the opportunity to incorporate new words into their writing. A good time for this is after pre-writing and before writing a first draft; another good time is after peer editing and before writing a second draft.

KINDS OF VOCABULARY STUDY

Strategies suggested in the Vocabulary Study Tools include grouping words into idea maps by concept; listing words according to parts of speech, for example, adjective, adverb, or noun; and setting up pairs of synonyms and antonyms. The Vocabulary Study Tools briefly model these approaches. Encourage students to experiment with these techniques.

SEQUENCE OF ACTIVITIES

Any or all of the following steps can be used to facilitate learning with the Vocabulary Study Tools:

1. Small groups or the whole class can generate a vocabulary list of 20 or more items. (During project work, it is helpful to use groups working on similar projects for vocabulary generation.)

2. Pairs of students can work together to categorize words by meaning (Vocabulary Study Tool Number 1) or by the part of speech (Vocabulary Study Tool Number 2).

3. Individual students can select five or ten words and list them on the Vocabulary Practice Sheets, using sentences useful for their drafts as example sentences.

4. Optionally, students can pick a few important words for their writing and search for synonyms and antonyms (Vocabulary Study Tool Number 3).

5. Students should try to incorporate five or more of the words studied into their writing.

Checklists

Students use checklists to review their drafts at the end of Units 5, 9, and 10 and for the Writing Projects throughout *Words in Motion.* To make effective use of these checklists, encourage students to follow them in order, ask questions if they are not sure what any of the instructions mean, and mark each step with a check mark (✓) when they complete it and before they go on to the next step.

Before assigning a checklist, preview it carefully in case you want to make modifications to fit your own procedures. You may decide in some instances to assign particular steps for class work and others for home-work. For example, you might tell students to "Work on steps 1 to 3 with a partner, then continue to follow steps 4 and 5 on your own. Complete steps 6 to 8 for home-work."

A reproducible Writer's Checklist is also provided in the Reproducible Resources section of this Guide for students to use in checking the second drafts of their writings before turning them in. You may want to introduce this checklist during Parts 1 and 2 of the book, but you will find it especially useful for Part 4. Copies of this checklist can be distributed with each assignment of a second draft, with the due date noted at the top. Have students hand in the checklist with their final drafts. This is a simple, clear, and fair way to hold students accountable for such details as format, title, name, date, and proofreading.

Checklists are used successfully in a variety of school contexts, from elementary and intermediate schools all the way through college-level writing classes. You can easily modify this Writer's Checklist to fit your individual teaching practices and assignments.

Grammar Clinic

The lessons in the Grammar Clinic are intended as a resource that can be used in a variety of ways to fit the needs and practices of particular classes and teachers. They cover a range of basic grammar and mechanics that will serve as review or reinforcement for most inter-mediate-level learners. The uniform design of all the Grammar Clinic lessons consists of one page of rule and example presentation followed by one page of exercises. Exercise pages all begin with Exercises for Practice that consist of structured practice, such as correcting exam-ple sentences or combining sentences. Most exercise pages also include an In Your Own Words exercise, which provides communicative practice, with questions that ask students to reply with sentences using the lan-guage structure being studied.

SELECTION AND SEQUENCING OF GRAMMAR CLINIC LESSONS

Five of the Warm Ups pages in the Student Book briefly review grammar points that are covered in the Grammar Clinic lessons, providing a built-in diagnostic and default selection of lessons. These references have been select-ed to be relevant to the writing tasks they accompany. You may wish to cover additional Grammar Clinic lessons when you feel they are needed, based on evalua-tion of your students' writing. In addition, in keeping with the book's intent to cultivate increasing learner awareness and learner autonomy, you may wish to sug-gest that students select those lessons that they will cover.

References to Grammar Clinic lessons in the units are the following. All references appear on Warm Ups pages unless otherwise specified:

Unit 1: Capitalization; Punctuation

Unit 4: Simple Sentences; Simple Sentence Patterns

Unit 8: Verb Tense Consistency

Unit 10: Simple Sentence Patterns; Complex Sentences

Unit 10: Page for Practice (footnote): Subject–Verb Agreement

Unit 12: Simple Sentence Patterns; Compound Sentences

The following Grammar Clinic lessons are not referred to in the units:

Listing Adjectives

Using Articles: *a, an,* and *the*

Pronoun Agreement

Use of Commas

STUDENT GROUPING AND GRAMMAR CLINIC LESSONS

As described below, Grammar Clinic lessons can be used with the whole class, with groups, or individually for homework.

1. *Whole class.* Either chosen as they come up in the Student Book, as they seem to be needed by your evaluation, or at student request, these lessons can be used as activities for the entire class.

    Introduce the lesson by writing several sentences on the board or overhead projector, all containing the same kind of mistake covered in the Grammar Clinic lesson. Make your own examples, or adapt them from the rules as presented in the book. Ask the students—working in pairs or small groups—to identify the mistakes and correct the sentences. Next, get students to report to the class and make corrections to the displayed sentences. Remind students that there may be more than one way to correct sentences, depending on the intended meaning. Then ask students, working in groups, to generate the rule needed.

    Now turn to the Grammar Clinic lesson and go over the rule presentation. You may wish to read the rules aloud and then ask students to read the examples aloud. Start the Exercises for Practice with the class, doing the first one on the board as an example. Answer any questions, then let students work alone or in pairs to complete the Exercises for Practice. Have students check their work with partners, and then provide their answers either on the board, orally, or by giving out copies of the appropriate answer key.

    If you have time, let students answer the In Your Own Words exercise as well. Otherwise, assign these for homework. To correct the In Your Own Words exercises, you can either collect the Student Books or ask the students to write the answers on their own paper so you can collect them.

2. *In groups.* If you are working with a mixed-level group of learners, you may wish to set up the class as a grammar lab, in which three or four groups work on different Grammar Clinic lessons. You can reproduce answers from this Guide and assign, or let students choose, groups according to their par-

ticular grammar needs. After a few such sessions, the most advanced students will either need additional grammar lessons to supplement the Grammar Clinic, or can work as tutors to assist the others working in groups and checking their In Your Own Words exercises. A mix of advanced lessons and tutoring will be rewarding for most advanced students. Such grammar labs, taking 30 to 90 minutes each, can be done on a regular basis, from three to six times during the course.

3. *Individually.* The Grammar Clinic may be best used as homework. You may want to assign particular lessons for individual students as you see the need. To make it fair for more advanced students, you may wish to assign them the task of looking for and marking examples of particular grammar usage, such as use of commas, complex sentences, or relative clauses, in English language novels or newspapers.

    Use the Grammar Clinic lessons as an ongoing reference and review resource. It is a good idea to reproduce and give students copies of the Mistake Log included at the end of this Guide to keep in their student notebooks along with their research, pre-writing, exercises, and drafts. After each second draft is returned, students can record the kinds of mistakes they made and the number of times each occurred. Based on this record, they can review the appropriate Grammar Clinic lessons right away and, especially, again before they finish the revision of their next major writing assignment.

General Teaching Suggestions for Units 1–12

Units 1 through 12 are each designed to be covered in one 60- to 90-minute class session, with the writing activity at the end of the unit finished as homework when needed. Of course, class levels vary, as do teaching styles, time available, and the constraints of the school's curriculum, and you may need to schedule the units differently to fit your own situation. The following suggestions for starting and finishing units should help you to get the most out of the book in a variety of situations.

STARTING A NEW UNIT

The suggested exercises that follow should be fairly brief; their purpose is to get students in the habit of previewing and predicting.

Each unit begins with a title page with an illustration and a list of the performance objectives of the unit. Before starting a new unit, it is a good idea to take advantage of both the illustration and the objectives to preview the activities that will occur within the unit.

Ask a student to read the unit title aloud. Direct the students' attention to the illustration and ask questions about it, such as, *What does this picture show? How do you think it is connected to the unit title? Who are these people? Where do you think they are? What do you think they are doing?* Discuss briefly with the class.

Then ask students to work in pairs to read the unit objectives and identify which ones are language skills and which are writing process skills. (You will probably need to define these terms.) Students should also skim through the four pages of exercises as they make their decisions about the objectives. For example, Unit 1 Goals: 1. Review punctuation and use of capital letters—*language;* 2. Practice taking notes and writing from notes—*writing process;* 3. Interview a partner and take notes—*writing process;* 4. Use vocabulary for writing about yourself—*language;* 5. Write without worrying about grammar—*writing process.*

Next, ask which unit goals are hard for students to understand (*which,* not *if*), and try to clarify any confusion. For example, in Unit 1 you may need to explain goal number five; the idea that we sometimes write without worrying about a finished product, just to develop our ideas by writing. If you have time, you could also ask students to find which pages focus on each of the goals.

CLOSING A UNIT

In many cases, especially in the units leading up to writing entire drafts, you may not be able to finish the activities on the Put It in Writing page within the class period. In such cases, you should make sure that students have read all the steps involved before the end of class and that they understand them.

Ask students to read the Put It in Writing page completely and to question you about any instructions they do not understand. Have the students work in pairs to come up with questions. Ask the pairs to report their questions. Answer the questions for the whole class.

Be clear about what you expect students to produce for the next class, and write it on the board so there is no confusion. (Students may need to meet in pairs for some activities.) Once the homework is clear, let students begin work on the activities in class, and help them with any questions or problems that come up.

Stop students at the end of class and tell them to finish the rest for homework. Make it clear, however, that any trading of papers or books and writing peer comments should be completed as an opening activity for the next class meeting.

Error Correction

Error correction is a difficult and sensitive issue in language learning, and especially in writing classes. Many students want to be corrected all the time, so they can "get it right." But having a composition returned full of red correction marks can not only be very discouraging, it can also be too overwhelming and unfocused to have much teaching value.

The basic approach to error correction in this book is to let students work without being corrected on grammar all the way through the drafting process, and to have mistakes marked only on their final drafts. Learners work on finding and correcting their mistakes as part of their own editing process before the teacher ever corrects their work.

The strategy also is to correct only those items that have been taught explicitly in class and have been announced, before the second draft is turned in, as "graded grammar points." The rationale for this is both to make error self-correction manageable for learners, and to test them only on what has been taught. For example, to test low-intermediate learners on subtle article or pronoun usage is self-defeating until they have control of more basic rules. (Some choices of articles or pronouns are rule-driven, but others are much more a matter of word choice.)

Learners may still ask you to correct all their errors all the time. Tell them the goal is for them to work on self-correction and develop greater awareness of their own mistakes gradually over the course of the school term. This will help them develop tools for learning independently. Let them know you want them to make clear progress on some grammar points rather than be distracted by trying to learn everything at once.

ERROR CORRECTION PROCEDURES

1. Let the students know that they will be asked to check their own writing for errors before turning in final drafts. Grammar, punctuation, and format points are introduced in Units 1 through 12 and can be reinforced with Grammar Clinic lessons as needed. Many of the exercises in the book and in the Grammar Clinic lessons involve error-correction practice.

2. After peer editing, remind students which grammar points have been covered so far, and let them know that their final drafts will be graded for errors on these items. Encourage students to check and correct such errors after revising for content, and again when proofreading, before they turn in their final drafts.

3. When you do correct errors, avoid simply crossing out and rewriting the mistakes for the students. This gives the students nothing to do and no way to really learn. It discourages rather than encourages grammar awareness. Instead, simply underline or highlight the errors. Ask the students to try to figure out the nature of the errors they have made, but be

prepared to answer questions if students can't tell for sure. You may prefer to use the correction symbols—found in the inside back cover of the Student Book and also included in the Reproducible Resources in this Guide—over the underlined errors.

4. When you return the papers, ask students to make sure they understand the nature of the errors and how to correct them. You can have students work in pairs to make sure they understand, while you circulate to answer any questions.

5. Give students copies of the Mistake Log (see page 62 of this Guide) and ask them to keep these in their notebooks along with their drafts and pre-writing notes. Give students some time to record on these logs the errors they made, including the kind of mistake, an example, and the number of times they made the same kind of mistake. You may also want to refer students to relevant Grammar Clinic lessons after handing back their drafts.

6. You will probably want to review with the whole class one or more basic errors that are common to many of your students. You may want to teach a specific Grammar Clinic lesson to the full class. Then, when students are ready to write their next second draft, you can review this point as one of the "graded grammar points" on which they need to guard against making errors as they produce their final drafts.

Another useful follow-up activity is to prepare an error correction exercise based on the common errors you want to focus on. You can base it on student writing, but alter it enough so that no one will be able to tell who wrote it—or, better yet, write your own. Let pairs and groups work on identifying the errors, then go over the answers with them, and assign an appropriate Grammar Clinic lesson for homework.

7. Finally, remember that the goal is to integrate grammar and error correction in a manageable way with the other aspects of writing, including communication goals, process, and creativity. Try to cultivate learner awareness and responsibility for finding mistakes, but do not hold students to a level so high that it guarantees failure. Language learning is a long and complex process. Focusing on rules and errors has its place, but it is only one part of the bigger picture.

Student Notebooks

A student notebook is a binder in which the student places all writings done outside of the Student Book. This includes drafts, pre-writing, research, reproducible resource materials, journal articles, quizzes, or other handouts you may distribute. Some students will also collect samples of real-world texts (materials such as movie reviews, pamphlets, letters, and so forth). Students who write and send letters will want to keep any replies received in their notebooks.

Organizing and keeping such a notebook up to date is a valuable study skill in itself. The notebook makes it easy to review the variety of language and writing skills practiced in the class, is an excellent place to keep track of one's errors—and one's progress—as documented by copies of finished writings and projects, and serves as a portfolio of the body of the student's work. Neat and well-organized student notebooks can help to build confidence as learners see the quality and quantity of work completed in English. For these reasons, the use of student notebooks is highly recommended.

Grading and Assessment

Like error correction, grading is a very sensitive issue. To avoid misunderstanding, your grading policy must be made very clear so that students know in advance what the game plan is. You may wish to negotiate the weight of various aspects of the class grade with your students, or prefer simply to announce it, but in either case it should be crystal clear to all.

It is a good idea to ask students to evaluate their own participation grade a few times during the term to encourage some reflection on their part. You will want to give some consideration to their perspective. As discussed above, the use of student notebooks is recommended , and you may wish to include assessment of them in your grading.

Here is a sample grading scheme for use with *Words in Motion*. You may wish to alter some of the categories and percentages, but in each case the figures should add up to 100. For example, if you choose not to grade student notebooks, homework and class assignments could then account for 40 percent of the grade.

Homework and class assignments	30%
Final drafts of writings and projects	40%
Participation in class, group, and pair activities	10%
Attendance	10%
Assembly of student notebook	10%
TOTAL	100%

GRADES FOR HOMEWORK AND CLASS ASSIGNMENTS

This category includes Learning Logs, Quick Writes, various kinds of pre-writing, research and interview notes, samples of writings (such as movie reviews) brought to class, Grammar Clinic lessons, first drafts, peer editing, revision markings and notes, and other specific assignments. A good way to grade homework is on a four point scale: check plus (✔+) = three, check (✔) = two, check minus (✔–) = one, and zero (0) = zero. Figure the grade as a simple percentage of the maximum total possible based on three points for each item, and then convert to 30 (or 40) points by multiplying it by .3 (30%) or by .4 (40%).

FINAL DRAFTS AND PROJECTS GRADE

These can be graded in four general areas:

Content—ideas and information	30 points
Organization	30 points
Grammar and Mechanics	30 points
Format	10 points
TOTAL	100 points

Each final draft thus has a maximum possible score of 100 points. Add the grades of all the student's final drafts together and divide by the total number of final drafts to get an average. Convert this to 40 points by multiplying it by 40 percent. For example a student writes five final drafts, with scores of 85, 88, 87, 90, and 95, for an average score of 89. Multiply this by .4 (40%), for a course grade for final drafts of 35.6 out of a possible 40.

Teaching
Words in Motion—
Unit by Unit

This section contains an overview of each unit, plus page-by-page suggestions (not prescriptions) for teaching the unit. Suggestions for pair and group work are included, but you should feel free to have additional exercises done by pairs or groups when you believe it would be helpful. Note also the following:

▶ Unless otherwise specified, all page numbers refer to pages in the Student Book.

▶ In the case of exercises containing several items, you may want to work through the first item orally with the class before assigning the remaining items.

▶ Answers to all exercises that are not open-ended are given in the Answer Key, which begins on page 43 of this Teacher's Guide. This Answer Key can be reproduced in whole or in part and distributed to the students for self-correction if desired.

▶ The verb "type" as in "have students *type* letters" is meant to include the use of a word processor or a computer as well as a typewriter.

Getting Started

Unit Overview

In this unit, students will:

▶ Review punctuation and use of capital letters

▶ Practice taking notes and writing from notes

▶ Interview a partner and take notes

▶ Use vocabulary for writing about themselves

▶ Write without worrying about grammar

RELATED STUDENT BOOK RESOURCES

Grammar Clinic lessons: Capitalization (page 97) and Punctuation—End of the Sentence (page 99).

SKILLS SUMMARY

Writing: Taking notes, writing from notes, Quick Write.

Language: Capitalization and punctuation.

Teaching Notes

WORK DUE?

No homework due. (You may want to review the Introduction to Writing on page viii before starting this unit, or just after it.)

GETTING STARTED

As a lead-in to this unit, ask students if they have ever:

1. stayed with a family in a foreign country

2. written a letter of self-introduction (in any language)

3. written a self-introduction to teachers or classmates

TEACHING SUGGESTIONS

Unit Opener (page 1)

See the discussion on pages 11–12 of this Teacher's Guide for suggestions for using the illustration and list of objectives.

Warm Ups (page 2)

Review briefly the use of capital letters in English and end-of-sentence punctuation in English. If students seem unsure, assign the Grammar Clinic lessons on pages 97 and 99 before doing the exercises.

Exercise 1. Have the class follow along as you read the directions aloud and be sure all students understand them. Call attention to the salutation which has

already been corrected. Tell the class that the handwritten answers show the way that they should make their corrections. Check that they understand what they are to do. Then work through the first paragraph with the whole class, eliciting each error and its correction (line 1, **I**, **s**tudent; line 2, **U**niversity; line 3, **A**merica; line 4, **E**nglish; line 5, replace the question mark with a period). Have the students do the remaining paragraphs independently. (The corrected letter is in the Answer Key.)

Exercises 2 and 3. Ask students to read the letter once more and then write answers to the questions. They do not need to write complete sentences. (Answers: 1. Mr. and Mrs. Weatherby; 2. No.)

Writing Matters (page 3)

Discuss the difference between the paragraphs and the notes in the two examples. Elicit that the notes contain only the most important words and are not in sentence form. Then have students write notes from the paragraph in Item 1. Have several students read their notes or put them on the board and ask for comments. When you are sure students understand how to turn a paragraph into notes, assign the remaining five items. (Suggested answers are in the Answer Key.)

Page for Practice (page 4)

Exercise 1. Read the instructions with the class and make sure they understand that they are to write answers about themselves in the column headed "Me."

Exercise 2. Divide the class into pairs, have them ask each other the same questions and write their partners' answers in the column headed "Partner." (The interview exercise can take a long time, so set a clear time limit and consider leaving the writing in Put It in Writing, page 5, for a homework assignment.)

Exercise 3. Working individually once more, each student writes two sentences about his or her partner, based on the notes taken in the "Partner" column.

Put It in Writing (page 5)

Exercise 1. See the discussion of Quick Writes on page 6 of this Teacher's Guide for suggestions for introducing this page. Some students may already be familiar with Quick Writing, but it may be a completely new idea to others, and especially to those who believe that everything they write must be as near perfect as possible. This particular Quick Write is not timed and can be done as homework if time is tight. If you can do it in the classroom, write with the students, writing as fast as you can, so they can see that you, too, can do it. **Exercise 2,** trading books, can be done in the next class if necessary.

HOMEWORK OR FOLLOW-UP

As suggested above, students can do the entire writing for homework and comment on each other's writing at the start of the next class. Or they can try another Quick Write without looking at their books or notes.

UNIT 2

Pre-writing

Unit Overview

In this unit, students will:

▶ Use specific information to add interest

▶ Practice making lists to get more information

▶ Make lists about themselves and their interests

▶ Use their lists to write about themselves

SKILLS SUMMARY

Writing: Writing lists, Quick Write, and writing peer comments.

Language: Writing *Wh-* questions.

Teaching Notes

WORK DUE?

No homework due unless student did the Quick Write from Unit 1 as homework. If so, partners should trade books and follow instructions for Exercise 2 on page 5.

GETTING STARTED

As a lead-in to this unit, ask students how they get ready to do any kind of writing, including letters, reports, essays, or any other genre, for example, making notes, drinking coffee, etc. After students give their answers, introduce list writing as a pre-writing tool for gathering specific information.

TEACHING SUGGESTIONS

Unit Opener (page 6)

Ask if any students do the kind of activity (windsurfing) shown in the illustration. Have them speculate on why it was chosen to open this unit. (The exercises have free-time activities as a theme.) Have students read and discuss the objectives.

Warm Ups (page 7)

Call attention to the examples, and discuss what is meant by the term "too general". Why is the first one "too general"? How does adding more specific information help?

Exercise 1. Call attention to the first item. Can students think of other questions? Then have them do items 2, 3, and 4. Call on volunteers to read their questions.

Exercise 2. Tell students that they can choose sentence 1, 2, 3, or 4 from Exercise 1 to rewrite. The sentence they write should include answers to their own questions.

Exercise 3. Have students answer the question. Emphasize the inclusion of specific details. Ask students, *Why does specific information make an answer to a question like this more interesting?*

Writing Matters (page 8)

Vocabulary may be a problem for students writing about hobbies and personal interests. You may want to let students spend time using a variety of dictionaries for the listing activity.

Exercise 1. Be sure students understand that each item in the box belongs in one and only one of the three lists in Step 3 of the example. (Answers are in the Answer Key.)

Exercise 2. This is pair work.

Page for Practice (page 9)

This page builds on the topics listed by the pairs in Exercise 2 on page 8, as students both narrow and expand their lists: narrowing by choosing only one topic from page 8, and expanding by adding subtopics and then listing specific items under these subtopics.

Put It in Writing (page 10)

Exercise 1. This is the students' second exposure to a Quick Write. For this one they should not use dictionaries. If they can't think of a word, tell them that they can leave a blank space. Emphasize once more that they are not to worry about mistakes. Call attention to the box with the Key Words and Phrases for Writing; tell them that this is to help them, but that they do not have to use any of the words or phrases if they prefer not to. Again, if it is feasible, do your own Quick Write as students are doing theirs. Have more paper available in the unlikely case that students run out of space. You may want to set a time limit of five or ten minutes for the Quick Write.

Exercise 2. Have the students write a *Wh-* question about their partners' Quick Writes.

HOMEWORK OR FOLLOW-UP

Extra (note at the bottom of page 10). Students can respond to their partner's question by writing more lists and another Quick Write on their own paper.

UNIT
3
First Draft

Teaching Notes

WORK DUE?

No homework due unless students did the extra Quick Write suggested at the bottom of page 10.

GETTING STARTED

As a lead-in to this unit, have students ask each other about their dreams for the future. Survey the future dreams in groups or with the whole class. (This unit will add the topic of plans for the future and get students ready to write a first draft.)

TEACHING SUGGESTIONS

(See the Answer Key for answers to the exercises.)

Unit Opener (page 11)

Discuss the illustration with the students. How do they usually write? In handwriting? Using a word processor or a typewriter? How many of them like to write the way the student in the photograph is writing? Discuss the objectives, with special attention to the last one. Elicit that the other objectives all deal with preparation of the draft they are going to write. Emphasize that this draft will not be a final product and that they will rewrite it later.

Warm Ups (page 12)

Exercises 1 and 2. Read the instructions for Exercise 1.

Then call attention to the box in Exercise 2. Make sure students understand the terms "double-spacing" and "indent." Point to the upper left blank and elicit that the word "name" from the box should be written in it. Have students fill in the other blanks, then hold up your copy of the book, point to each blank, and have individuals tell you what word or words belong in it.

Exercise 3. Paragraph indention and double-spacing are standard for writing in English classes, but may be new to students from other cultures. Exercise 3 recognizes this and serves to emphasize that this is the way students should write their compositions in this class.

Writing Matters (page 13)

This page deals with the "anatomy" of a composition and emphasizes that all compositions have an opening, a body, and a closing—that is, a beginning, a middle, and an end.

Exercises 1 and 2. Have students read the examples in Exercise 1. Call special attention to the three Notes below the box. Then have them circle and label the relevant parts of Alice's composition in Exercise 2. (Answers are in the Answer Key.)

Exercise 3. Have students follow the instructions, circling words or phrases they think they could use in writing about themselves and comparing these with a partner.

Page for Practice (page 14)

This page continues the emphasis on the three parts of a composition and suggests words and phrases that might be used in a self-introduction.

Exercise 1. Do the first item with the class, and establish that it belongs in the closing of a self-introduction and therefore the letter **C** should be written in the blank. Then have students complete the exercise, writing **O, B,** or **C** in the proper blanks. Go over the answers with the class (see the Answer Key).

Exercise 2. Dictionaries may be useful. Any words looked up can go onto a vocabulary worksheet or into the student's notebook.

Exercises 3 and 4. The sentences written in these exercises can form part of the draft that students will write at the conclusion of the next page.

Put It in Writing (page 15)

See the discussion of checklists on page 10 of this Guide. This page gives students their first experience of writing a first draft from a checklist. Let students write the draft (or finish it) on their own paper for homework, but make sure they understand how the checklist works (they must do the steps in order and check as each is accomplished) before the end of the class. Be sure to tell them that they will use the first draft in the next class, and ask them not to forget to bring it to that class.

UNIT 4

Editing

Unit Overview

In this unit, students will:

▶ Look at what is and what is not a sentence

▶ Learn questions and symbols for editing

▶ Practice editing a composition for interest

▶ Edit the first draft their partners wrote in Unit 3

RELATED STUDENT BOOK RESOURCES

Grammar Clinic lessons: Simple Sentences (page 103) and Simple Sentence Patterns (page 105).

SKILLS SUMMARY

Writing: Writing peer comments.

Language: Sentences and sentence fragments.

Teaching Notes

WORK DUE?

Students must have their first drafts from Unit 3 to participate in this activity. (In case one or two have forgotten their drafts, you can have them work on writing their drafts from memory in class and they can do peer comments on each other's drafts for homework.)

GETTING STARTED

As a lead-in to this unit, ask students if they have ever asked someone to look at their writing (in any language) and comment on it.

TEACHING SUGGESTIONS

Unit Opener (page 16)

Call attention to the title of the unit and have four students read the four objectives aloud. Ask what students think the word "editing" means. Elicit that editing is a way of helping a writer to communicate better by raising questions and suggesting changes. Discuss how the illustration relates to the objectives.

Warm Ups (page 17)

Exercise 1. Have the class read the instructions. Then work through the first item with them. Elicit that the correct answer is *d, subordinate clause.* Have the students complete the exercise individually.

Exercises 2 and 3. Have students, still working individually, underline the fragments in the letter and rewrite two of these fragments as complete sentences. Call on individual students for their revised sentences, and ask for comments or alternate versions from the class. (Answers are in the Answer Key.)

Writing Matters (page 18)

Read the definition of peer editing at the top of the page. Explain or elicit that the word "peer" means an equal, so peer editing is editing by a friend or partner instead of by a teacher or other person in authority. Explain that there is a difference between correcting grammar and improving content in writing. On page 17, students worked on a grammar point to help them with their own writing, but here they will edit only to help their partners with content. They will not be formal teachers to each other, but helpers. (Most professional writers get help from friends and editors with writing.) Work through the example with the students, pointing out how the words and symbols at the top of the page have been used by the peer editor. Call attention to the question, *What does "hick" mean?* Elicit or explain that the adjective "hick" is used to refer to a place that is out in the countryside and is simple and unsophisticated.

Exercises 1 and 2. Put the students in pairs and have them edit the paragraph at the bottom of the page, using the words and symbols in the box. Then have them write questions to ask for specific information that will make the paragraph more interesting.

Page for Practice (page 19)

Exercise 1. Students now edit a longer composition, using the words and symbols they learned on the preceding page.

Exercise 2. Students compare their editing marks with a partner. Finally they complete the four items of Exercise 2, giving their own opinions about the composition.

Put It in Writing (page 20)

Students now trade books and first drafts and edit their partners' writing.

Exercise 1. Be sure they fill in both names as requested; these are helpful for record keeping.

Exercises 2 and 3. Students use the words and symbols they have learned (which are repeated here) to edit their partners' drafts. Then they complete the comment sentences below. Students should not "pull their punches," but they should be positive, not negative, in their statements. Provide more paper if they want to write more than there is space for on the page.

Exercise 4. Students get their own drafts back, read the comments, and ask partners about any comments they don't understand. (This is what the students in the photograph on page 16 are doing.)

HOMEWORK OR FOLLOW-UP

Students could finish the peer comments at home if they need more time. If the peer comments are finished, students can answer their partners' questions and try making more lists or doing a Quick Write.

Be sure students understand that they must bring their first draft and peer comments to the next class session!

UNIT 5

Second Draft

Unit Overview

In this unit, students will:

▶ Use markings to make it easy to rewrite

▶ Revise a composition for organization

▶ Look at how content should suit their reader

▶ Practice revising and rewriting

▶ Revise their own compositions about themselves

RELATED STUDENT BOOK RESOURCES

Grammar Clinic lessons that have already been completed. Revision symbols from Unit 4 (pages 18 and 20) and peer-editing comments from Unit 4.

SKILLS SUMMARY

Writing: Revising, writing a second draft, and proofreading.

Teaching Notes

WORK DUE?

Students must have their first drafts and peer comments for this lesson. (If they don't, they can do the first four pages of the unit, but they will have to revise and rewrite their draft later.)

GETTING STARTED

As a lead-in to this unit, have students ask each other how they can improve their first drafts. Get a sampling of these ideas reported back to the class.

TEACHING SUGGESTIONS

At this point, you may have a few students who are behind in the process. Let them do the activities in this unit until the Put It in Writing page. After that, they will need to work on catching up.

Unit Opener (page 21)

Call attention to the title and the illustration. Ask, *What is the student at the computer probably doing?* (Writing a second draft.) Have students read the objectives and discuss them. Call attention to the second and third objectives. Ask, *What is meant by organization?* Ask,

How could you make your content suit the reader? What would you need to know first? (Who the intended reader is.)

Warm Ups (page 22)

Discuss the purpose of revision markings and how this differs from the purpose of the editing markings they learned in Unit 4. (Revision is something you do to improve your own writing; peer editing is something someone else does to help you improve your writing.) Have students study the revision markings.

Exercise 1. Have the students follow the markings on the sentences and rewrite them accordingly.

Exercise 2. Have the students compare their rewritten sentences with their partners' and make corrections if necessary. Then have each student answer the question. In the full class, call on individual students for their answers and ask them the reason(s) for their choice.

Writing Matters (page 23)

This page addresses the second and third unit objectives and asks students to think about both organization and the intended reader or audience.

Exercise 1. If there is time, you may want to have students compare, with partners (or with the class, using an overhead projector), where they have relocated the underscored sentences.

Exercise 2. Again, if time permits, a sampling of students might read their answers to the question aloud to the class.

Page for Practice (page 24)

Exercises 1 and 2. Read the instructions aloud with the students. Draw special attention to the two directions. Be sure students understand that what they are doing is revising this piece of writing by substituting information about themselves for the information about the original writer. They are using the revision markings introduced on page 22 to mark up Carolyn's paragraph (direction 1), and they are making notes about what to say about their own hometown (direction 2).

Exercise 3. Students now write their revised paragraph which, except for the added information about their hometown, should be a mirror image of Carolyn's, sentence for sentence, but with all the information personalized to become information about themselves.

Put It in Writing (page 25)

Before having students do this page, you may want to review once more the discussion of checklists on page 10 of this Guide. Students may be able to start their revision and rewriting in class, but they will have to finish this for homework. Make certain that students have time to read the checklist and to ask questions before the end of the class. Also, it is very important that you tell students what you will be grading for before they write the second draft. For example, you might tell them that you will be grading for *content*—ideas, *organization*—composition structure and format, and those specific grammar points that they have studied in class.

HOMEWORK AND FOLLOW-UP

Students write their second drafts. A good follow-up activity is to let students trade papers and read each other's drafts before they turn in their second drafts.

Tell students to be sure to bring all their lists, drafts, and other written work to the next meeting of the class. They will need these as they fill out the Learning Log on page 26.

Learning Log for Part 1

To fill out the Learning Log for Part 1 on page 26, students should have all the written work, both in the Student Book and on their own paper, that they have done in Part 1. See the discussion of Learning Logs on pages 7–8 of this Guide. The Learning Log form looks deceptively simple, but students need to take it seriously if they are going to benefit from it.

If students are keeping notebooks, you may wish to make photocopies of this Learning Log and have them fill these out rather than mark their answers in the Student Book. They can then keep their Learning Logs in their notebooks. The Learning Log for Part 1 is included in the Reproducible Resources section of this Guide.

Exercise 1: Think back: Students read the short review of Part 1, circle the activities or topics they enjoyed the most, and underline the skills which they want more help with.

Exercise 2: Look back: Students look through the pages of Part 1 to remember the activities and see their work again. Because these pages are part of the historical record of each student's development as a writer, students should make no changes on them now.

Exercise 3: Write about it: Students answer the two questions to tell you—and themselves—more about their progress.

Vocabulary Notes: Students note any vocabulary they want to remember from Part 1. They will want to look at the lists they made in Unit 2 and the vocabulary they used in all the units of Part 1. If they are using the Vocabulary Study Tools (see pages 67–71 of this Guide), they may want to consult these and be sure that the words on this section of the Learning Log also appear on their vocabulary worksheets.

Collect the individual Student Books or the photocopied Learning Logs. Tell students that they will be graded only on whether they made an honest effort to answer the questions. Return the books or Learning Logs at the next class session.

Writing Project for Part I

Project Overview

Before assigning this first Writing Project, you may want to reread "Writing Projects" on pages 8–9 of this Guide. Both the Project Sheet and Project Skills pages are set up as checklists. Be sure that students follow the sequence and that they check each step as it is completed.

RELATED STUDENT BOOK RESOURCES

Writing Sample of a Personal Profile (page 86), note-taking exercise in Unit 1, peer editing in Unit 4, and revision markings in Unit 5.

GETTING STARTED

For an extended lead-in to this project, ask students to bring in articles in English about famous people. These can be from magazines, books, or newspapers. Trading these samples around a group is a good way to get students interested and provide models.

For a quicker lead-in, you could ask students to write down names of famous people they respect and also names of friends or acquaintances whom they respect. Students can work with partners to ask each other about the people they listed.

TEACHING SUGGESTIONS

This project can be large or small, depending on the ability of the class and how much time you spend on it. If you don't have much time, keep the project to a single class session plus one or two days outside of class. Set firm dates for each phase of the project, and make sure students report their progress at some fixed points along the way. Make the students responsible for negotiating any exceptions to your deadlines. The interviewing of the chosen subject will, in almost all cases, need to be done outside of class. It is a good idea, however, to allow class time for some or all of the actual writing so students understand that the project is just as important as the units of the book. Be sure to be available to help students solve problems. You might even devote some time to group or whole-class work where students can discuss problems and solutions for finishing their project.

Project Opening page (page 27)

Ask the class what they think is happening in the photograph. Why is the standing woman holding a microphone? Elicit that she is interviewing the seated woman and is going to write about her. Then read, or have a student read, the description of Writing Projects above the photograph and discuss it. Ask students to turn quickly to the Project Sheet page (page 28) as you read the three descriptive sentences about it below the photograph on page 27; do the same with the Project Skills page (page 29). Tell students that these pages will help them as they complete this first Writing Project.

Project Sheet (page 28)

Introduce the term "personal profile," and tell students that they are going to write one. Point out that the steps on this page will carry them through the entire production of their personal profile. Step 4 may be the most time-consuming, since students may have difficulty finding interesting people who are willing to take the time to be interviewed. Step 6, as mentioned above, will probably have to be done outside the classroom, perhaps in the subject's home or place of employment and at a time convenient to him or her.

Project Skills (page 29)

Writing Tip 1. Call attention to the box at the top of the page and remind students of the similar box on page 7. Elicit that specific details are always more effective than general statements. In this instance, the specific details "tell a story," which grabs the reader's interest, as does the opening sentence of the sample profile on page 86.

Writing Tip 2. Emphasize to the class the absolute importance of quoting a person's own words in direct quotations—this is made easier by use of a tape recorder as shown in the photo on page 27. If students use indirect quotations, they should be sure that the ideas expressed are those of the interviewee, not of the interviewer!

HOMEWORK OR FOLLOW-UP

Some of the writing may need to be done as homework, especially the production of a second draft after peer editing. Let students know that they will be graded on only the grammar points taught in Part 1.

A simple follow-up is a read-around, in which students pass their drafts around in a small group, read each other's projects, and ask and answer questions about them. Another possibility is to make a small booklet of the completed projects—if you have the time and if you and the class agree that they are worth collecting.

UNIT 6

Friendly and Formal Letters

Unit Overview

In this unit, students will:

▶ Look at language for formal and informal letters

▶ Learn the structure for a formal letter

▶ Practice correcting a formal letter

▶ Choose a letter they want to write

▶ Write a draft of their own formal letter

RELATED STUDENT BOOK RESOURCES

Writing Samples: Information Letter (page 88) and Envelope (page 95).

SKILLS SUMMARY

Writing: Awareness of differences between formal and informal letters and among letters written for different reasons and for different readers.

Language: Formal and informal language for letters.

Teaching Notes

WORK DUE?

No homework due, unless some students have not yet handed in their completed Personal Profiles.

GETTING STARTED

As a lead-in to this unit, have pairs of students ask each other who they usually write letters to and if they get letters from overseas. Ask pairs to report to the class.

TEACHING SUGGESTIONS

Unit Opener (page 30)

Have students talk about the illustration. Then have them read the five objectives. Ask what the terms "formal" and "informal" mean to them. To whom would they write a formal letter? To whom an informal one?

Warm Ups (page 31)

Exercise 1. Have students check the boxes: the left hand letter is formal, the other, informal. You may want to ask on what basis students made their decisions.

Exercises 2 and 3. Do the first box (Topics) with the whole class; next have students complete the chart,

filling in the other boxes. Then have them complete the sentence in Exercise 3.

Writing Matters (page 32)

This page presents two different formats for formal letters, but each includes the same basic information.

Exercise 1. Review the names of the different parts of a letter in the box at the top of the page. The terms "return address," "inside address," and "salutation" may be unfamiliar to the students. Have students write the number of each part next to that part in the two formats.

Exercise 2. Have students read the four rules and cross out the wrong one (which is the second one). Poll the class to find out which one they crossed out and ask why they crossed it out.

Exercise 3. This is pair work. Have pairs give their answers.

Page for Practice (page 33)

Be sure students complete **Exercise 1** before going on to **Exercise 2.** Check the answers by calling on students to tell you what they circled and asking the class if they agree. Then have students use the revision symbols from page 22 to correct the letter. The words and phrases in the box can be used as replacements for items that are unsuitable for a formal letter.

Put It in Writing (page 34)

Exercises 1 and 2. Here the students write their own formal letters. Be sure they answer the two questions in Exercise 2 before actually writing the letters.

Exercise 3. The addresses in the box were correct at the time this book was written, and sincere letters should get a reply. You may want to bring in some additional newspaper and/or magazine ads for other places to write to.

Exercise 4. After students have written their letters, have them trade with a partner and mark the part that shows the letters' main purpose.

The **Extra** option for students to type their letters will take more time, requiring you to check their letters more carefully. To add to the coverage of formal letters, you may want to ask students to bring samples of business letters in English and spend time looking at the format and language—if you have time and your students are interested.

HOMEWORK OR FOLLOW-UP

A simple follow-up would be for students to neatly rewrite their letters by hand. A more demanding follow-up would involve pairs or groups working together to type their letters or print them out using a word processor or computer and mail them. The **Extra** option is a third possibility.

UNIT
7

Setting the Scene

Unit Overview

In this unit, students will:

▶ Look at the form of one kind of friendly letter

▶ Use language for describing a place

▶ Practice writing about a picture

▶ Try a Field Study to write about a place

RELATED STUDENT BOOK RESOURCES

Writing Samples: Pen Pal Letter (page 87).

SKILLS SUMMARY

Writing: Describing places. Writing peer comments.

Language: Using adjectives and spatial-order words and phrases.

Teaching Notes

WORK DUE?

Any extra or follow-up work from Unit 6 should be completed and handed in before you start teaching Unit 7.

GETTING STARTED

As a lead-in to this unit, have students work in groups to ask each other the reasons they write cards and letters to friends or families. Let the groups report to the whole class.

TEACHING SUGGESTIONS

Unit Opener (page 35)

Have students read the unit title and look at the photograph. Ask if any of them recognize it (the Imperial Palace in Tokyo, Japan). Then ask them what they think the unit is going to be about (writing descriptions). Ask them to read the four objectives. Call attention to the fourth one, and ask, *Does everyone know what a field study is?* Elicit or explain that the students will be going outside the classroom to another site and writing a description of that site.

Warm Ups (page 36)

This page concentrates on the friendly letter, one kind of informal letter.

Exercise 1. Point out that friendly letters are written

for many reasons. Call attention to the box below the letter, which lists six of these. Read the instructions with the class and have them check which of the reasons in the box best fits the letter, which is to keep in touch with a friend.

Exercise 2. Have students reread the letter and answer the questions by checking the appropriate boxes (1. second paragraph; 2. third paragraph; 3. first paragraph).

Writing Matters (page 37)

Read the statement at the top of the page, and point out that in Jim's letter on the preceding page, he described both the scene from his window in Tokyo and the places he visited in Thailand, giving lots of specific details. Call attention to the illustration on this page and the three details given as examples. What other statements might students put in a letter about this scene, if they were telling someone about it in a letter?

Exercise 1. Have students complete three sentences about the classroom. Urge them to give specific details to make the room "come alive" to the reader.

Exercise 2. Have students write sentences about their own rooms at home. The list of spatial-order words and phrases is intended as help—students are not required to use all of them. Have more paper available if students want to write more than there is room for on the page.

Page for Practice (page 38)

Exercise 1. Pair work. Students work with partners, thinking of ways to describe what is going on in the picture. Be sure they have paper on which to make notes and lists. Be sure also that they understand that the Questions to Ask and Answer box is there to help them, not to restrict them.

Exercise 2. Now working individually, students take their notes and write sentences about the picture. Provide additional paper if needed.

Exercise 3. Explain that adjectives can make their sentences more interesting. The Hints box suggests some, but there are many more they could use. You might want to brainstorm some of them before students do the activity.

Put It in Writing (page 39)

This page is preparation for writing a field study. Students have described pictures, now they are going to write a description of a completely different place.

Exercises 1 and 2. The students start by choosing the location they will go to. They are asked to write down three possible locations, since they can't be sure that their first choice will be appropriate when they get there.

Exercise 3. Then they practice by describing, with a partner, where they are "right now," using words in the box to help them.

Exercise 4. The actual field study is to be done outside the classroom, in one of the places they chose, and submitted as homework in the next class session. Note that this field study is done as a Quick Write and will be graded accordingly, that is, grammar and spelling will not be taken into account in the grading.

NOTE: If circumstances make it impossible for students to leave the school to do a field study, you may wish to pass around postcards or pictures from travel magazines and have students write the field studies as if they actually were in those places.

HOMEWORK OR FOLLOW-UP

As suggested above, the Field Study itself is the homework. Emphasize that students must bring their Field Study to the next class session.

UNIT
8
Telling a Story

Unit Overview

In this unit, students will:

▶ Review verb tense in writing

▶ Practice using time-order words and phrases

▶ Make a story from pictures

▶ Write and edit their story

RELATED STUDENT BOOK RESOURCES

Grammar Clinic lesson: Verb Tense Consistency (page 115).
Writing Samples: Scary Story (page 91).

SKILLS SUMMARY

Writing: Telling a story or narrative; writing peer comments.

Language: Using time-order words and phrases.

Teaching Notes

WORK DUE?

Students should bring in their completed field studies from Unit 7.

GETTING STARTED

As a lead-in to this unit, briefly tell students a story about a trip you took. Tell students they will work on telling a story in English in this unit. (Alternatively, let pairs of students read and comment on each other's field studies.)

TEACHING SUGGESTIONS

Unit Opener (page 40)

Call attention to the title and illustration. Discuss what is shown. If students were there, is this something they would like to tell someone about? Why? Then have students read the objectives. Ask how the first two objectives are connected to telling a story, and point out that the last two show that they are going to write a story themselves.

Warm Ups (page 41)

Have students look at the examples. Ask why the first "Not Consistent" sentence is incorrect. Elicit that "yes-

terday" shows that the person is talking about past time, but the verb "will go" is in the future tense. Work through the other two examples in the same way.

Exercise 1. Have students read the letter and underline the sentences with mistakes in verb tense.

Exercise 2. Have students check answers with a partner and write corrected versions of two of the incorrect sentences.

Writing Matters (page 42)

Discuss with the class how the time-order words underlined in the brief story help to make clear what the person did and when she or he did each part.

Exercise 1. Have students read the words in the box before they write their description of what they did "this morning, last night, or last weekend."

Exercise 2. After they have finished writing and have underlined the time-order words and phrases, ask if there are places where using more of these might make the sequence even clearer.

Page for Practice (page 43)

On this page, students are challenged to do guided story making. It is guided in that they must incorporate elements from three of the pictures into their story ideas, but how they do this is entirely up to them. Although this activity asks students to "work with a partner," you may wish to have it done by groups of three or four students rather than by pairs in order to stimulate more expression of ideas. (In either case, the actual story writing on page 44 is to be done by individuals.)

It is important that students understand that this is an *imagination* activity: there are no "right" or "wrong" answers. Students are to use their creativity to think of possible connections among the three pictures they choose. Their story ideas need not be serious or "sensible": they can be funny, scary, or just plain wild. Students should let their imaginations run free as they plan their story ideas.

Exercise 1. Go over the instructions orally with the class. Emphasize that each pair (or group if you select that option) can choose any three of the pictures, and that they can use these three pictures in any order to make up a story idea that connects the pictures in some way. Tell them that their story idea can be funny or serious, that it can be a mystery or an action story or any other kind of story. The only rule is that the story should show some connection among the three pictures. Then have the pairs or groups choose their pictures and start working out the story orally.

Exercise 2. Have the students write notes about their story idea. (They will use these notes later when they actually write the story.) This activity can take a long time. Give pairs or groups a time limit to keep them on task (for example, 10 minutes to talk and 10 minutes to write notes).

Put It in Writing (page 44)

Exercise 1. Students work individually to write their stories, using the notes they wrote on page 43. Read the instructions with them before they start: Emphasize the use of time-order words and phrases, and emphasize also the freedom to change information and ideas as they go along. Let them know that they can use more paper if necessary to complete their stories.

Exercise 2. When they have completed a draft of the story, have them follow the editing steps. The partner in Step 4 should not be the partner (or group member) with whom the story idea was worked out on page 43, but after Step 4, the original partners may wish to compare stories. If time is short, you can let students finish this writing page for homework. They can read and comment on each other's work in the next class.

HOMEWORK OR FOLLOW-UP

As noted above, students can write (or finish writing) and edit their stories for homework and then read and comment on each others' stories in the next class. If students did finish and comment in the last class meeting, they can trade books with different partners in the next class meeting and see what kind of stories other students wrote.

UNIT 9

Writing a Letter to Keep in Touch

Unit Overview

In this unit, students will:

▶ Look at language for a friendly letter

▶ Study the format for a friendly letter

▶ Study a "recipe" for a letter to keep in touch

▶ Gather ideas for their own letter

▶ Write a draft of a friendly letter

RELATED STUDENT BOOK RESOURCES

Friendly letter (page 36).
Writing Samples: Pen Pal Letter (page 87).

SKILLS SUMMARY

Writing: Parts of a friendly letter. Awareness of audience, writing notes, and telling a story.

Language: Language for writing a friendly (informal) letter.

Teaching Notes

WORK DUE?

If students did not complete their stories in Unit 8, they should bring them to this class session, trade stories, and write their comments on their partners' stories. If this applies to only some of the students, the others can read different partners' stories and comment on them.

GETTING STARTED

As a lead-in to this unit, ask students to work in pairs or groups to list the main skills they studied in Units 7 and 8. List answers on the board. They should include describing a place and telling a story. Explain that they will use those skills to write a letter in this unit.

TEACHING SUGGESTIONS

Unit Opener (page 45)

Have a student read the title aloud. Remind the class that they have already read a "letter to keep in touch" on page 36. Elicit that the person in the illustration may be writing this kind of letter. Have the students read the

objectives. Ask how students will go about "gathering ideas" for their letters (objective 4).

Warm Ups (page 46)

Exercise 1. Discuss with the class how the form of a friendly letter differs from that of a formal letter. You may want to have them return briefly to page 32. Notice the lack of return address and inside address in the friendly letter. What other differences do they see? Then read the instructions with the class and demonstrate drawing a line from the words "Greeting or salutation" to the greeting on the letter form. Have them complete the remaining items.

Exercise 2. Point out that not only the forms of the friendly letter and formal letter differ, the language also differs. Read the instructions for the exercise, than ask the students to look at item 1. Ask, *Why is there an x in the first box? Should there be x's in any other boxes?* (Dear Sir or Madam:) *There is a check mark in one box: what other boxes should be checked?* (What's up buddy?) Note that "Good night," and "Please note:" are not marked either way, since neither is a greeting or salutation. Have students continue with items 2 and 3.

Writing Matters (page 47)

Exercise 1. Ask students if they ever follow a recipe when they are making something to eat. You may want to bring in a recipe from a magazine or newspaper and show how it lists ingredients first and then gives instructions in order. Tell them that this page is a recipe for writing a letter to a friend. It starts with a list of ingredients—items that will go into the letter—and continues with a list of instructions called Writing Steps. Their task is to decide which ingredients belong in which parts of the letter by writing the letter of the right part next to each ingredient, and then to number the Writing Steps to show which comes first, second, and so on.

Exercise 2. Students now decide who they will write to. One good way to let students write to each other is to have them write their names on small strips of paper, fold them, and then mix all the papers so students can pick names at random. Alternatively, you can arrange for your class to exchange letters with another writing class.

Exercises 3 and 4. Students practice the list making they learned in Unit 1 as they arrive at topics for their letters.

NOTE: The "recipe" given here is only one of many ways to write a letter. Let students know that this is a useful formula, but not a universal rule or convention.

Page for Practice (page 48)

Exercises 1 and 2. Students continue with their listing and note making in preparation for writing their letters. Exercise 2 asks for specific details; let students use dictionaries and also tell them that you are ready to give vocabulary help.

Put It in Writing (page 49)

The checklist takes the students step by step through the writing of their letters. Urge them to follow every step and to look at each page referred to for examples and suggestions. Students will probably write their drafts for homework, but make sure that they read and understand the checklist during the class. And be sure to highlight Step 7: Bring the completed draft to the next class session.

HOMEWORK OR FOLLOW-UP

As mentioned above, students will probably need to write (or finish) the draft of their letter outside of class. They will peer edit each other's letters in the next class.

Revising Your Letter and Writing a Final Draft

Unit Overview

In this unit, students will:

▶ Practice combining short sentences

▶ Practice editing for interest

▶ Edit the draft a classmate wrote in Unit 9

▶ Edit their own drafts for interest and form

▶ Revise and rewrite their own drafts of a letter

RELATED STUDENT BOOK RESOURCES

Grammar Clinic lessons: Simple Sentence Patterns (page 105), Complex Sentences (page 109), and Subject-Verb Agreement (page 113).
Writing Samples: Pen Pal Letter (page 87) and Envelope (page 95).

REPRODUCIBLE RESOURCES

Writer's Checklist (page 61 of this Guide).

SKILLS SUMMARY

Writing: Peer editing for content, self-editing for form, revising, and rewriting.

Language: Sentence combining with prepositional phrases and subordinate clauses.

Teaching Notes

WORK DUE?

Drafts of the letter to keep in touch from Unit 9. Those who have not completed their first drafts will need to do so before beginning to work on page 52.

Getting Started

Tell students that they are going to revise and rewrite the drafts they wrote in Unit 9. This unit will help them with new strategies for writing, editing, and revising.

TEACHING SUGGESTIONS

Unit Opener (page 50)

Ask students what the illustration shows (an outdoor concert). Have any of them ever attended such a concert? Tell them that they will read part of a letter about

this kind of leisure-time activity as they learn about more kinds of editing. Then have them read the objectives. Ask students what they think the difference is between editing for interest and editing for form. Answer any questions they have about the other objectives.

Warm Ups (page 51)

Read the introductory statement with the class. Go over the examples in detail, eliciting how the meaning of each of the short sentences is included in the longer, combined sentence. If necessary, review the difference between prepositional phrases and subordinate clauses. Elicit that a clause has a subject and a verb (but is not a sentence), while a phrase does not.

Exercises 1 and 2. Work through the first item with the class. Accept either "Maria went home by taxi after midnight" or "After midnight Maria went home by taxi." Then have students do the remaining items in Exercise 1 and all those in Exercise 2. If students have difficulty with these, you may want to use with the whole class the Grammar Clinic lessons cited at the bottom of the page.

Writing Matters (page 52)

Review the peer editing that students have already done (for example, on pages 18 to 20). Remind students that peer editing is not correcting mistakes, but helping to improve content.

Exercise 1. Give students time to read this segment of a letter carefully, and ask them to comment on it. Are there other editing marks or comments they might want to put on it?

Exercise 2. Pair work. Partners now trade the first drafts of the letter they wrote in Unit 9 and peer edit it for interest—not for form and grammar; they will do this later themselves. Make sure students don't peer edit letters written to them. Change some partners if necessary—they should read the letter for the first time when they finally receive the second draft.

Exercise 3. Students get the letters back and look at their partners' editing marks and comments. They should make at least four changes as a result of the editing.

Page for Practice (page 53)

Exercises 1 and 2. Students now practice editing for grammar, punctuation, and format. Using the sample in Exercise 1 and the editing correction symbols, they edit the writing samples at the bottom of the page. If time allows, call on individuals to tell you what they marked and why, and ask students for comments and/or additional changes or corrections.

Put It in Writing (page 54)

Again, students use a checklist to self-edit, revise, and rewrite their letter to keep in touch.

NOTE: Peer editing (page 52) may take a long time. Try to finish page 53 (Page for Practice) and make sure students have time to read and understand the checklist on page 54 before the end of class. Have students bring two copies of their completed second drafts—one for you and one, with an envelope, to deliver to their readers.

HOMEWORK AND FOLLOW-UP

Students will write their second drafts for homework. The follow-up is when students deliver the letters to their readers in the next class. They could possibly also write brief replies if there is time.

Learning Log for Part 2

To fill out the Learning Log for Part 2 on page 55, students should have all the written work, both in the Student Book and on their own paper, that they have done in Part 2. You may want to review again the discussion of Learning Logs on pages 7–8 of this Guide. Remind students that the Learning Log is there to help them; they should take it seriously and think carefully about their responses if they are to benefit from it. As suggested for the Part 1 Learning Log, if students are keeping notebooks for this course, you may wish to have them use photocopies of this form. See the Part 2 Learning Log in the Reproducible Resources section of this Guide.

Exercise 1: Think back: Students read the short review of Part 2, circle the parts they liked most, and underline the skills they want more help with.

Exercise 2: Look back: Students look through the pages of Part 2 to remember the activities and see their work again. Remind students not to make any changes on this material.

Exercise 3: Write about it: Students answer the two questions to tell you—and themselves— more about their progress.

Vocabulary Notes: Students note any vocabulary they want to remember from Part 2. Urge them to look at every page of Part 2 for new words. If they are using the Vocabulary Study Tools (see pages 67–71 of this Guide), they may want to consult these and be sure that the words on this section of the Learning Log also appear on the vocabulary worksheets.

Collect all of the Student Books or the photocopied Learning Logs. Remind students that they will be graded only on whether they made an honest effort to answer the questions. Return the Student Books or Learning Logs at the next session.

Writing Projects for Part 2

Part 2 has two writing projects. Students can choose either the Pen Pal Letter or the Information Letter, or try both if they have time. If this comes just before a vacation and you are short of time, you can skip these projects completely, or let students find people and places to write to during the vacation so they can do their letters soon after school starts again.

GETTING STARTED

As a lead-in to these projects, survey the class to see who has pen pals and who has taken part in study or travel programs abroad. Let students ask each other questions and then collect information from the whole class. Next, let students look at the two projects and choose the one they want to do. Have them look at the photograph on page 56. Ask, *What is this person doing? What kind of letter do you think this person is going to write?* Elicit that she is studying advertising material from different schools or colleges and will write to one or more of them to get additional information.

Project A: Pen Pal Letter

Project Overview

RELATED STUDENT BOOK RESOURCES

Writing Samples: Pen Pal Letter (page 87). (Students may already have read this while working on Units 9 and/or 10, but may wish to refer to it again at this time.) Envelope (page 95).

REPRODUCIBLE RESOURCES

Writer's Checklist (page 61 of this Guide).

Teaching Suggestions

The crucial part of this project is finding a pen pal. Unless there is a local pen pal organization, it may take time to find one. You may want to arrange for a letter exchange with another school (such as an international school), or have students write to inquire about pen pals instead. Once students have pen pals to write to, give them time to work in class (or have them do it as homework). You may want to suggest that they keep

brief notes on their progress in the form of diary entries with date, time spent, and work done.

Be sure students use the Writing Project and Project Skills pages (pages 57 and 58).

Writing Project (page 57)

This page is in checklist form. Tell students to read all the steps first before doing any of them, and then to do the steps in order. Step 1 can be omitted if students have just read the pen pal letter on page 87. Discuss Step 2 briefly, making sure that students understand the various sections of the letter. Note that in Step 3, they skip to the next page to do the exercises there, then return to Step 4 on this page. Ask students to think about Step 5. Why is this an important step? How much do you need to know about your reader? How much *can* you know about your reader if this is the first letter you are writing to her or him? The answers will vary depending on who the pen pal is and how he or she was discovered.

You may want to ask students to make two copies of the final, revised letter in Step 8 (probably as homework). Collect one copy of the letter, and have students mail the other copy to the chosen recipient. (Refer them to the sample envelope on page 95 in the Writing Samples section.) Tell students they will be graded on only the grammar points taught in Parts 1 and 2.

Project Skills (page 58)

Writing Tip 1. This relates directly to Step 5 on the previous page. **Writing Tip 2.** This raises questions of style and culture. Discuss the example with the class. Why is the question about religion "too personal"? Have students look at the five questions. You may want to do all of these with the whole group doing this project. In most Western or Western-influenced cultures, questions 1 and 4 would be considered too personal.

HOMEWORK OR FOLLOW-UP

Writing of the letter, and especially the final draft (Step 8 on page 57) may need to be done as homework. Before students send their letters, you may want to have them share the letters in groups. Students can make a class log of who sent letters where and who received answers.

Project B: Information Letter

Project Overview

Students write a letter to ask for information about study or travel.

Teaching Suggestions

Writing Project (page 59) and Project Skills (page 60)

Page 59 is in checklist form. Tell students to read all the steps first before doing any of them, and then to do the steps in order. Students may need some time to do research outside of the classroom while doing Step 4. It may be a good idea to encourage students to work in pairs or small groups for this information gathering. If possible, arrange to visit a library and/or an English language bookstore.

If students did not send letters to either of the institutions named on page 34 of the Student Book, they might want to do so as part of this project. These addresses were current at the time this book was written. Page 60 contains additional addresses that may be helpful.

Check all letters in final form before students send them out to make sure that no errors or omissions have crept in at this last stage.

HOMEWORK OR FOLLOW-UP

Writing of the letters, and especially of final drafts (Step 8 on page 59) may need to be done as homework. Before students send their letters, you may want to have them share the letters in groups. Students can make a class log of who sent letters where and who received answers.

Once letters are ready to send, be sure to keep copies (possibly in a class file or notebook) and set up a log of places written to, including names and dates. This way, you can complete the class file or notebook with copies of replies as they come in.

Ideas and Paragraphs

Unit Overview

In this unit, students will:

▶ Look at paragraphs and topic sentences

▶ Read samples of tourist guides

▶ Use idea bubbles to organize ideas

▶ Write from idea bubbles

RELATED STUDENT BOOK RESOURCES

Writing Samples: Tourist Pamphlet (page 89).

SKILLS SUMMARY

Writing: Topic sentences and paragraphs. Pre-writing with idea bubbles. Writing from idea bubbles.

Teaching Notes

WORK DUE?

If students completed their Part 2 Writing Project as homework, this is the time to bring it in, show it to you, make last minute corrections, and send it out.

GETTING STARTED

Tell students that this unit will deal with travel pamphlets. Ask students to name a few interesting places to visit, either in their country or abroad, and list a few of them on the board. Discuss what makes these places appealing. If students were going to write a pamphlet for tourists about one of these places, what would they put in it? Tell them that in this unit they will make a start on such a pamphlet.

TEACHING SUGGESTIONS

Unit Opener (page 61)

Ask students if they know where the photograph was taken. Elicit or tell them that it was taken in California in a national park called Yosemite (Yo-SEM-it-ee). They will be reading a paragraph about this park. Then have them read the objectives. Ask them what they think idea bubbles are (objectives 3 and 4); let students know that they are a way to organize ideas before writing. Answer any questions they may have about the objectives.

Warm Ups (page 62)

Read the opening statement with the class. Students have been reading and writing paragraphs throughout Parts 1 and 2, so the first sentence is in the nature of a review. The concept of topic sentences, however, may be new to many students, although others may have learned it in their study of reading in English. More often than not, the topic sentence is the first sentence of the paragraph, but sometimes it comes later. Call attention to the box at the top of the page. Elicit that the "focus" tells something important about the topic: It is the main point of the topic sentence.

Exercise 1. This exercise can be done either individually or in pairs. Have students read the article on Yosemite National Park. You may want to show them where it is on a map. If there are words students don't understand, tell them to look them up later. Tell students they are to divide the article into three paragraphs by writing a circled P where they think each paragraph should begin. Point out that the first P has already been placed at the beginning of the article. Work with the whole class to locate the second P (after ". . . something for everyone."). Let individuals or pairs locate the third one by themselves (after ". . . at the visitor's center.").

Exercise 2. If students did Exercise 1 as individuals, have them compare their answers with a partner. Then, as individuals, have them circle the topic of the first sentence (the topic sentence) of each paragraph and underline the focus words. (Answers are in the Answer Key.)

Exercise 3. Ask the students to think about a city or tourist location that they are familiar with and write a topic sentence about it. The topic will be the name of the place and the focus will be what is special about the place ("beautiful beaches and rich culture" in the example at the top of the page). The Yosemite article may be a fertile source of vocabulary words that students will want to organize in their notebooks or on vocabulary worksheets.

Writing Matters (page 63)

This page introduces the pre-writing strategy called idea bubbles. Tell students that the organization of ideas and important facts in a topic they want to write about can be diagrammed in idea bubbles. The incomplete idea bubble diagram on this page shows the organization of facts and ideas in the article "Festival City" at the top of the page. The students' job is to read the article and then fill in the empty bubbles. On later pages, they will write from an idea bubble diagram and then make their own idea bubble diagram and write from it. As with Yosemite, you may wish to show where Edmonton is on a map or globe.

You may find it necessary to guide the class through filling one or more of the empty bubbles. For example, elicit that the top right bubble should contain "over 400 restaurants," since that is the fact in the article that is not accounted for in the cluster of "international foods" in the diagram. The remaining empty bubbles can be filled by students working either individually or in pairs. Expect that some students will take much longer than others to complete this page. Be ready to answer questions and to provide help and guidance if necessary. This article, like the earlier one, is a good source of vocabulary that may be new to students.

Page for Practice (page 64)

Ask the class what they know about New York City. Can they locate it on a map of the United States? Elicit or explain that New York City is very large, with five counties (known as "boroughs") of which Manhattan (New York county) is the smallest but the best known.

Exercise 1. Ask the class to read the paragraph about Manhattan and look at the idea bubbles below it. Elicit (or explain if necessary) that the idea bubbles contain much more information than the paragraph. Tell the class that one part of the idea bubbles was used to write the paragraph. Have them find and circle the upper left cluster, the main bubble of which reads "all you want in NY on a small island." Ask two or three students to find and read an individual bubble, for example, "13 miles long" and then find and read the sentence to which that bubble contributed. ("Only about 13 miles long. . . .") (This particular sentence is based on three bubbles.) Elicit that the bubbles represent facts and ideas, not final wording.

Exercises 2 and 3. Students now use idea bubbles to write from. For Exercise 2, they choose another part of the diagram—"great theaters and performances," "famous sites," or "world class museums"—and write a topic sentence about that part, using the bubbles as a guide. Then for Exercise 3, they do the same thing again. These exercises assume some knowledge about New York City. Make sure your students at least recognize most of the places named. Supply information if needed. The main point is to help the students develop interesting and well-formed topic sentences; you may want to encourage them to look back at the two preceding pages for models.

Exercise 4. Here students are asked to evaluate their topic sentences. It is a good idea to let stronger

and weaker students work together on this. Circulate as they work, giving suggestions as needed. If time permits, put examples on the board. You may also want to put an example of a poor topic sentence (made up by you so as not to embarrass anyone), such as "New York also has museums." This example does not give enough information to focus the topic; let students suggest ways to improve it.

Put It in Writing (page 65)

Exercise 1. Students now make their own idea bubbles diagram, then use it to write a paragraph for visitors. This involves three clear steps: (1) They choose a city or tourist attraction to write about. This may be the same one they chose in Exercise 3 on the Warm Ups page (page 62) or it may be a different place. It is important that students know enough about the place to be able to write an interesting paragraph about it. (2) On their own paper, students make an idea bubbles diagram of facts and ideas about their chosen place. You will want to circulate and check to see that this is done properly, with subtopics and facts arranged to show the relationships among them. Remind students that these idea bubbles are for one paragraph, not a complete multi-paragraph article. (3) Students write their paragraphs.

Exercise 2. Students write a concluding sentence about the best time to visit their chosen location.

Exercise 3. Students trade books with partners and read and write comments on the partners' paragraphs.

NOTE: Emphasize to the class that these paragraphs are first drafts. Students are not expected to produce a final peer- and self-edited product in this unit or in Unit 12. The emphasis here is on writing a well-organized paragraph with an interesting topic sentence. A more polished form of the paragraph might be used in the Tourist Pamphlet Writing Project in Part 4, if the student chooses that option.

HOMEWORK OR FOLLOW-UP

If time is running short, you may wish to assign the actual writing of the paragraph on page 65 (Step 3 of Exercise 1) plus all of Exercises 2 and 3 as homework.

UNIT 12

Ideas and Opinions

Unit Overview

In this unit, students will

▶ Review compound sentences

▶ Practice using words to mark their ideas

▶ Read samples of movie reviews

▶ Use idea markers to write about a movie

RELATED STUDENT BOOK RESOURCES

Grammar Clinic lessons: Simple Sentence Patterns (page 105) and Compound Sentences (page 107). Writing Samples: Movie Review (page 90).

SKILLS SUMMARY

Writing: Using idea markers. Writing compound sentences.

Language: Movie review vocabulary.

Teaching Notes

WORK DUE?

If students completed their tourist pamphlet drafts for Unit 11 as homework, they should bring these in now, trade them with their partners, write comments, and give them to you.

GETTING STARTED

Write the word *OPINION* on the board and underline it. Ask, *What is an opinion?* Write answers on the board as they are given and ask for comments or corrections. Then ask, *How does an opinion differ from a fact?* Elicit that a fact is something that can be proven. For example, the statement that *Rebel Without a Cause* starred James Dean and Natalie Wood is a fact. An opinion is someone's personal idea about something. The statement that *Rebel Without a Cause* is one of the best movies ever made is an opinion. Movie reviews are statements of the reviewers' opinions, although they may sometimes include facts as well. Tell students that in this unit they will be looking at a movie review and an article about a movie and ways that opinions and facts are organized in them.

TEACHING SUGGESTIONS

Unit Opener (page 66)

Call attention to the illustration. Do students know what it is? (A still from *Rebel Without a Cause*.) Are they familiar with the movie? What was their opinion of it? Good? Bad? So-so? Tell them they will read a short review of it later. Then have them read the objectives. Call attention to the last one. What do they think an "idea marker" is? Write their answers on the board and tell them that they will find out about, and use, idea markers as they go through the unit.

Warm Ups (page 67)

Read the opening statement. Be sure everyone understands that an "independent clause" is another term for a sentence. It becomes an independent clause when it is joined with another independent clause to form a compound sentence (or with a dependent clause to form a complex sentence). Work through the examples with the class. Some students may have been under the incorrect assumption that all compound sentences have "and" in the middle; the opening statement and the examples introduce the other conjunctions "or," "so," and "but."

Exercise 1. Read the instructions with the class. Note that a comma is to be used before any conjunction that students use to fill the blanks. (In some simple compound sentences, commas are unnecessary for meaning, but they are never incorrect and using them in every compound sentence is a helpful habit to develop.) Work with the class to fill the first blank ("and"), then have students work independently to fill the others.

Exercise 2. Read the directions. Ask which conjunction the class will use in the first item (either "and" or "but" is acceptable). Have them write the sentence and then do the other items independently.

Writing Matters (page 68)

Read the definition of idea markers at the top of the page and work through the examples with the class. Call attention to the three categories: words or phrases that signify an additional idea, words or phrases that signify a contrasting or opposite idea, and words or phrases that signify sequence or order. You may want to point out that while all the idea markers in the examples are the beginning words of sentences, idea markers can also be found within a sentence. Also point out that not every idea marker is listed on the page. For example, "another" and "yet another" are listed, but "other" and "the other" are not. Elicit or provide additional examples of idea markers if this seems appropriate at this time.

Exercise 1. Go over the instructions with the class. Students are to choose whether to write an "adding" or a "contrasting" idea marker to start their new sentence in each item.

Exercise 2. Here students use idea markers to show the order of ideas. Have them read through the entire brief article before filling in any of the blanks. Then work with the class to fill in the first blank (either "First of all" or "First"). Students can work individually or with partners to fill in the remaining blanks.

Page for Practice (page 69)

Exercise 1. Tell the students that here they will be looking for the idea markers in a review of *Rebel Without a Cause,* the movie from which the illustration on page 66 was taken. (Although it was made more than 40 years ago, *Rebel Without a Cause* is still popular. Students who are not familiar with it may want to rent it to view at home.) Have students read the review and circle all the idea markers. Do the first one as a whole class. Students should circle "However," at the beginning of the second sentence. Then let them work in pairs or individually to find and circle the others.

Exercise 2. This exercises gives students practice in thinking about and writing down information about a film that will be useful in writing a review of that film. Students can work in pairs or, if they prefer, individually or in small groups to answer the questions and list the strong and weak points of the movie. Call attention to the box at the bottom of the page: these are words commonly used in writing about movies, and students may wish to put them on their vocabulary worksheets and/or use them in their review.

Put It in Writing (page 70)

Exercises 1-4. Students now write a draft of a movie review. Tell them they should follow the three pre-writing steps before doing any actual writing, making an idea bubbles diagram as the last of these steps. Call attention to the second sentence in the instructions for Exercise 4: "Use the idea markers you practiced in this unit." You may want to suggest that they look again at the way idea markers were used in the review of *Rebel Without a Cause.* The review that the students will write, like the tourist pamphlet material in Unit 11, is a draft, not a finished, peer- or self-edited piece of writing. If students are interested, they may want to try a movie review as one of their projects in Part 4 (see the **Extra** note at the bottom of page 70).

HOMEWORK OR FOLLOW-UP

You may want to have students do the actual writing of their draft outside of the classroom and bring it to the next class session.

Teaching
Words in Motion—
Part 4: Project Writing

Part 4 Overview

In Part 4: Project Writing, students will:

▶ Try a variety of writing projects in a variety of genres

▶ Choose the writing projects they want to do

▶ Choose whether to work alone or with a partner

▶ Choose the kinds of pre-writing they want to use

▶ Use editing and revision skills to rewrite projects

RELATED STUDENT BOOK RESOURCES

Project and Goals (page 72)

Project Log (page 73)

Project Planning Form (page 74)

In addition, there are two pages each for the following writing projects:

Movie Review (pages 75–76)

Tourist Pamphlet (pages 77–78)

Scary Story (pages 79–80)

Speech (pages 81–82)

Résumé and Application Letter (pages 83–84)

The first page of each, headed Writing Project, is a checklist of steps to be taken to complete the project. It also includes a diagram of the format of the project. The second page, Project Skills, contains Writing Tips and Project Tips, which include exercises dealing specifically with the particular project.

Teaching Suggestions

Preparing for Part 4

Before beginning Part 4, it would be helpful to review the discussion of "Writing Projects," beginning on page 8 of this Guide. Part 4 has a very flexible format, which allows students to work independently or in pairs on projects they choose themselves. The time that your class spends on project work will vary with the number and extent of the projects the students choose.

By Part 4, your students should be familiar with the writing process and with a variety of genres of writing in English. They will also be familiar with what is meant in this book by the term "writing project" if they worked through the projects at the ends of Parts 1 and 2.

Student Choices

Choices are a key element in project work. Each student can pick a project according to his or her own interests. For example, the Movie Review project (page 75) might be chosen by students particularly interested in the media or entertainment. Students interested in studying overseas or applying for a job requiring English proficiency might find the Résumé and Application Letter project (page 83) more relevant.

Other decisions students will make, after consultation with you, concern whether to work alone or in pairs, what kinds of pre-writing exercises and editing and revision strategies they will use, and whether to attempt more than one project. While the final decisions should be made by the students, you will want to provide help and guidance: students do not always find it easy to make choices.

Choices and the Classroom

Since students choose the projects they want to work

on, different students may be working on each of the five projects at the same time. As long as the subject matter and focus of each student project are unique, there is little problem with students copying from each other. However you may want to require that no two students review the same movie or guide tourists to the same site or attraction. You may also want to require that each student do at least one project individually (not as part of a pair) in order to make sure that everyone takes responsibility for her or his own work and earns her or his own grade. A possible way to satisfy this requirement in a small class is to have all students write movie reviews individually as a first project, then let them choose freely from the remaining four projects. (In large classes this may be impractical because of the number of different movies needed.)

All the projects *except* the Résumé and Application Letter can be done in pairs, but to encourage individual responsibility and accountability, you may wish to limit the number of projects that are co-written.

Classroom Management

Like group activities, project work creates a workshop-style classroom in which individuals and pairs are working on their projects independently of each other—and you. Even when students are working on different projects or at different stages of a project, however, you can maintain some of the advantages of a teacher-led classroom by starting and ending each class session with a brief teacher-led activity, such as a Grammar Clinic lesson or vocabulary work. Another way to bring the class together is to ask students to exchange projects, on the day they are due, with new partners for questions and comments. You can close some classes by putting a common problem on the board, eliciting solutions from the class, and, if necessary, offering your own suggestions.

Grading and Assessment of Projects

Grading project-work is similar to grading the 12 units (see the discussion of "Grading and Assessment" on page 13 of this Guide). Completed Project Logs, Project Planning Forms, Project Skills exercises, drafts (except for the final one), and any assigned vocabulary work or Grammar Clinic lessons can be graded as homework. The finished Writing Projects can be given full letter grades.

One way to avoid having to check every project step—and to make students more autonomous—is to have students keep all their work, from pre-writing and information gathering to all drafts, in their notebooks. You can still check some homework to keep students on track, but at the end of the term you can collect all the notebooks and give a grade based on the quality, quantity, and organization shown in them.

Finally, you will probably want to give some percentage of credit on the basis of class participation. Depend-ing on your class, you might want to consider letting students grade themselves on their participation.

Integrating Project Work into the Curriculum

If your writing program is part of a larger English curriculum, consider coordinating at least one Writing Project with that curriculum. For example. the Speech project would fit well with a conversation or speech-class unit on discussion, a class on politics or current events, or a schoolwide speech contest. Likewise, the Résumé and Job Application project could go along with a typing, computer, or Business English class.

Projects and the Real World

Too often, anything done in the classroom is considered unrelated to the real world. This doesn't have to be so. For example, some students might write application letters and résumés to apply for summer jobs in English-speaking countries or at the offices of American or English companies in their country. Perhaps one or more local temples, museums, historic areas, or shopping districts would like a tourist pamphlet in English, or a local theater catering to speakers of English would appreciate having new reviews of classic movies. A brainstorming session with the class may produce other real-world suggestions for turning the project writing experience into more than just an academic exercise.

Teaching Part 4

Use the project planning pages (pages 72, 73, and 74). Their purpose is to raise students' awareness of the kinds of material the projects deal with, the writing skills involved, and the purpose, audience, and specialized vocabulary needed. They also provide a place to log in the projects the students work on.

The two-page lessons for each project are simple and clear. The first page is a checklist with a diagram or visual format showing the main sections of the finished piece of writing. The second page presents tips and exercises directly related to the content of the project. You will probably want to work through one of these pairs of pages with the whole class simply to show them how to proceed. It should not be necessary to go through all five, although you may want to be sure the students follow the checklist steps, which include doing the exercises on the second page, when they undertake a new project. The Résumé and Application Letter pages deviate slightly from this pattern, in that each of the two pages is similar to the first page of the other projects and there are no exercises—other than writing the résumé and the application letter.

Again, before you assign any projects, please reread the discussion of "Writing Projects" on pages 8–9 of this Guide for more information on planning and managing this important part of *Words in Motion*.

Words in Motion
Answer Key

This Answer Key may be reproduced in whole or in part for self-correction by students if desired. You can mask out unwanted material by covering it with a piece of white paper before photocopying a given set of answers.

Answers are included for all pages and exercises for which there are "correct" answers. *Those pages or exercises for which no answers are provided here either do not have written answers (for example, checklist pages) or have only open-ended questions or items for which answers will vary widely, depending on each student's interests, preferences, experiences, and other factors unique to that student.*

Exercises that do not have "correct" answers are often more useful for evaluation of student progress and achievement than those that do. Check such exercises carefully, both for appropriateness and to make sure that students have understood and followed the instructions and, especially, for students' feeling for the English language and their basic understanding of how it works.

UNIT 1

Getting Started

Exercise 1

(Changes to be made by the student are <u>underlined</u> *and set in* **boldface** *type. Students will actually make these changes by crossing out the error and writing the correction above it. The only punctuation errors occur at the end of the salutation and at the end of the first paragraph.)*

Dear Mr. **a**nd Mrs. Weatherby**,**

My name is Midori Tanaka. **I** am 20 years old and a **s**tudent of Temple **U**niversity, Japan. For many years, it has been my dream to be an exchange student in **A**merica. While I have studied **E**nglish for more than seven years, I have never traveled outside of Japan**.**

I'd like to tell you a little bit about my background. I grew up in a small town in northern Japan. There were many rice fields near my **h**ome and beautiful views of the mountains. I have an older brother, Junichi, and a younger sister, Naoko. **M**y mother and father like sports, so our whole **f**amily often went cycling or played tennis together. These days, I live in a dormitory, and I miss my mother's cooking and our **d**og, Cookie!

I hope **I** can learn a lot about American life and culture from you. Of course, I'll try to tell you about **J**apan as well. I'm still not very good at understanding **s**poken English, so please speak slowly to me. I look forward to meeting you.

Exercise 2

(Accept short forms, unless you requested complete sentences.)

1. (She's writing to) Mr. and Mrs. Weatherby.
2. No, (Midori hasn't met them).

Exercise 1

(Answers will vary. Here are some possibilities.)

1. Vicki—collected postcards in H.S., cards from many countries
2. Wilbur—ethnic food—Indian, Thai, Greek
3. Susan—grew up Sydney—H.S., usher in opera house
4. Ralph—part time video rental—likes, sees movies free
5. Julia—home stay program, Seattle 9 months
6. Kim—big family, traditional Chinese house

Pre-writing

PAGE 7

Exercise 1

(Answers will vary. Here are some possibilities.)

2. What do you do at the beach? Which beaches do you go to? Who do you go with? How often do you go? How do you get there?

3. What kind of videos do you like? Where do you watch them? Who do you watch them with? What are your favorite videos? Do you also like to go to the movies sometimes?

4. What do you like to cook? What kind of foods are your favorites? Who do you cook for? Do you use a cookbook? How did you learn to cook? How long have you been cooking? How often do you cook?

PAGE 8

Exercise 1

Under "guitar": guitar lessons, music group, songbook.

Under "sewing": blouse for Mom.

Under "windsurfing": wet suit, sunscreen.

U N I T

3

First Draft

PAGE 12

Exercises 1 and 2

(Answers at left of model.)	*(Answers at right of model.)*
name	date
indent	title
	double-spacing
left margin	right margin

PAGE 13

Exercise 2

Opening: "I'd like to introduce myself. My name is Alice, and I'm from Massachusetts."

Body: "I grew up in Rockport . . . . My dream is to work for a big company and live in Spain."

Closing: "Well, I think I'm going to enjoy this writing class. I look forward to getting to know you this semester."

Exercise 1

C I hope to meet . . .

O Let me introduce . . .

C Please tell me about . . .

B Another one of my interests . . .

B My hometown is . . .

O I'd like to tell you . . .

B When I was in high school . . .

C I hope to hear . . .

O My name is . . .

U N I T
4

Editing

PAGE 17

Exercise 1

1. d   2. c   3. b   4. a

(Since Fragment 3 has no verb; either b or c would be correct.)

EXERCISE 2

Fragments:

1. Because my father changed jobs.
2. Where I play tennis on Sundays.
3. Especially old, romantic movies like "Gone with the Wind."
4. Apple pie and brownies, too.
5. Because I can't understand English very well.

PAGE 19

Exercise 1

Answers will vary, but check to see that correct questions and symbols were used.

U N I T
5

Second Draft

PAGE 22

Exercise 1

In 1989, I moved to Los Angeles. That is where I went to high school. These days, I live in a small apartment with my mother, father, sister, and a little black dog named Ralph. When I get home, my dog is always waiting to go for a walk.

PAGE 23

Exercise 1

(Underlined sentences are shown where they belong. Accept alternate placements if students can justify them.)

I'd like to introduce myself. My name is Jiang and I grew up in Hong Kong. My family moved to Portland, Oregon, two years ago. I've been studying at Portland Community College for six months now, and I've been lucky to meet many friends here.

In addition to my studies, I have a part-time job in a hamburger restaurant near campus. I'm a cashier. It's difficult, because I have to work late sometimes, and then it's hard to wake up in time for school. I also don't like wearing the uniform and little hat. Still, I really like the people I work with. I've made some good friends this year. Of course, I'm also saving money for a trip next summer.

My interests include sports and travel. In my free time, I like to play soccer. I'm not on a team, but there is usually a pickup game on the big field at school in the afternoons. In the winter, I like to go skiing in the mountains. Last January, I took a ski trip to Mount Hood with some friends.

My dream for the future is to be an electrical engineer. First, I plan to study engineering at the University of Washington in Seattle. Some day, I hope to work for a computer company in Taiwan. That's my story. I look forward to hearing your story too.

PAGE 24

Be sure students have converted the sentences to be true of themselves and have answered the question, "Can you tell me more about your hometown?"

Writing Project for Part 1

PAGE 29

Writing Tip Exercise 1

Check (✓) should go before sentence 1. (Sentence 2 is too general.)

Writing Tip Exercise 2

(Answers will vary. Here are some possibilities.)

1. "I wanted to study literature, " Akiko said, "and I wanted to renew my energy."
2. Akiko said she wanted to go to America because she wanted to study literature and renew her energy.

Friendly and Formal Letters

PAGE 31

Exercise 1

Dear Ms. Clinton: ✓ formal
Dear Susie, ✓ informal

Exercise 2

	Topics	Greeting or Salutation	Special Vocabulary	"Be" Verbs and Contractions	Punctuation
Formal Letter	job application, résumé, interview	Dear Ms. Clinton:	(on chart in Student Book)	I would, I am, I have, I will	(on chart in Student Book)
Friendly Letter	(on chart in Student Book)	(on chart in Student Book)	Hey, thanks, great, wow, glad, crazy, dorm, etc.	(on chart in Student Book)	Dear Susie, *(Students may add !)*

Exercise 3

The purpose is to get a job interview and then to get a job as a tour guide.

PAGE 32

Exercise 1

(for both letters, from top to bottom): 1, 2, 3, 4, 5, 6, 7, 8.

(1. return address; 2. date; 6. closing; 7. signature; and 8. typed name are on left in full block, on right in semi-block.)

Exercise 2

The second rule, "Tell about your favorite childhood memory and your hobbies" is wrong and should be crossed out.

PAGE 33

Exercise 1

*(Changes to be made by the student are <u>underlined</u> and set in **boldface** type. Accept reasonable alternate words or phrases.)*

> **<u>Dear Sir or Madam:</u>**
>
> I'm **<u>going to</u>** visit your city, and I **<u>would like to request</u>** some information on sightseeing and hotels in Sydney.
>
> Since I plan to visit in March, **<u>I would</u>** like to get some ideas about what to see or do at that time of year. I **<u>would appreciate</u>** some pamphlets, maps, and other information about the Sydney area. **<u>Please</u>** send **<u>any information</u>** to me at the following address:

327 Post Street, Apt. 7B

San Francisco, CA 90502

Thank you in advance for your **assistance.** I look forward to hearing from

you soon.

Sincerely yours,

Tim Coulmas

Tim Coulmas

U N I T

Setting the Scene

PAGE 36

Students should make check marks as indicated.

Exercise 1

✓ to keep in touch with a friend

Exercise 2

1. ✓ 2nd
2. ✓ 3rd
3. ✓ 1st

U N I T

Telling a Story

PAGE 41

Exercise 1

Verb tense mistakes:

1. Last weekend, I **go** canoeing. . . .
2. . . . so we **can** get an early start.
3. . . . and **are parking** near an old wooden bridge. . . .
4. . . . we ate some sandwiches and **will drink** a cup of coffee.
5. Then we put the canoe in the water, **get in,** and started down the river.

The five corrected sentences (students choose two to correct) are as follows:

1. Last weekend, I **went** canoeing with a friend from school.
2. I spent the night at Mike's house on Friday so we **could** get an early start.
3. After another hour, we got to a wide valley with a winding green river and **parked** near an old wooden bridge.
4. Before starting our trip, we ate some sandwiches and **drank** a cup of coffee.
5. Then we put the canoe in the water, **got** in, and started down the river.

UNIT

9

Writing a Letter to Keep in Touch

PAGE 46

Exercise 1

Greeting (small top left oval); Body—opening (upper rectangle); Body—closing (lower rectangle); Closing (small lower right oval).

EXERCISE 2

Friendly letter (mark with ✓):

1. "Dear Midori," "What's up buddy?" (very informal)

2. "Thanks for your fascinating letter." and "Sorry I haven't written for so long." and "As I write this, I am sitting in a small café."

3. "Yours truly," "Bye-bye" (very informal), "With all our sympathy," "Sincerely," (and for a very close friend) "Love and kisses."

Too formal (mark with an "x"):

1. "To whom it may concern:" "Dear Sir or Madam:"

2. "I am writing in regard to . . ." and "I am writing to request information . . ."

3. "Respectfully yours,"

PAGE 47

Exercise 1

Ingredients	Writing Steps
a	2
a	6
b	1
b	3
b	5
c	4

(Accept reasonable alternatives.)

UNIT

10

Revising Your Letter and Writing a Final Draft

PAGE 51

Exercise 1

(Suggested sentences. Accept reasonable equivalents.)

1. Maria went home by taxi after midnight.
   OR After midnight, Maria went home by taxi.

2. Six business people were singing in front of the train station.
   OR In front of the train station, six business people were singing.

3. After work, Larry fell asleep on a bench in Seaview Park.
   OR Larry fell asleep on a bench in Seaview Park after work.

Exercise 2

1. The telephone rang after Jerry fell asleep.
   OR After Jerry fell asleep, the telephone rang.

2. Sally went into a cafe where a lot of young people were talking.
   OR A lot of young people were talking in a cafe where Sally went.

3. The bell rang before Steve finished the exam.
   OR Before Steve finished the exam, the bell rang.

4. Rick got angry when Tim and Suzie danced the tango.
   OR When Tim and Suzie danced the tango, Rick got angry.

PAGE 53

Exercise 2

"I wants" S/V
"collegge" SP
"sunday" C
"come" VT
"sea" SP
"person" **OR** "man" unnecessary (retain either "person" or "man" but not both)
"to went" VT
"the and" reverse word order

Writing Projects for Part 2

PAGE 58

Writing Tip 2

Questions 1 and 4 are too personal.

UNIT
11

Ideas and Paragraphs

PAGE 62

Exercise 1

New paragraphs:

1. "Yosemite National Park is a place . . ."
2. "Yosemite Valley offers a variety of . . ."
3. "The high country of the Park offers . . ."

Exercise 2

1. *topic:* Yosemite National Park; *focus:* a place filled with wondrous natural beauty for all to enjoy.

2. *topic:* Yosemite Valley; *focus:* a variety of comfortable ways for travelers to enjoy the park.

3. *topic:* The high country of the park; *focus:* enjoyment and challenges for more adventurous travelers.

Exercise 1

Seven items are to be filled in:

> *Under "the Works":* Visual Arts Celebration
>
> *Under "festivals every summer":* latter half of July
>
> *Under "Klondike Days Extravaganza":* parades *and* raft races (two items)
>
> *Next to "early August":* Fringe Theatre Event
>
> *Next to "1st Sat. & Sun. in August":* Heritage Days
>
> *Next to "international foods":* over 400 restaurants

PAGE 64

Exercise 2

The upper left section of the bubbles should be circled ("all you want in NY on a small island" and the bubbles radiating from it and the ones radiating from them).

UNIT 12

Ideas and Opinions

PAGE 67

Exercise 1

1. and
2. but
3. or

(Check to see that each is preceded by a comma.)

Exercise 2

1. Harrison Ford is great in action movies, and he's good at comedy, too.
2. Science-fiction movies are popular, but not everybody likes them.
3. I can't afford to go to movie theaters, so I rent videos of older movies.

PAGE 68

Exercise 1

(Answers may vary. Here are some possibilities.)

1. However, documentaries are sometimes more interesting.
2. In contrast, others like dramatic films.

Exercise 2

1. "First of all" **OR** "First"
2. "Second" **OR** "Next"
3. "One more"
4. "Another" **OR** "Yet another"
5. "Finally"

(Accept reasonable alternatives.)

Exercise 1

(Paragraph 1) "However"

(Paragraph 2) "The other" "Then" "More"

(Paragraph 3) "One thing" "Another thing" "On the contrary"

(Accept reasonable alternatives.)

Part 4: Project Writing

PAGE 72

Exercise 1

Project	Text Type	Writing Skills	Purpose
Movie Review	. . . magazine . . . newspaper		. . . introduce. . .
Tourist Pamphlet		describing a place, . . .	
Scary Story	short story	. . . , telling a story	. . . entertain. . .
Speech			. . . opinion
Résumé and Application Letter	. . . formal letter		. . . employer. . .

PAGE 78

Writing Tip

1. Change "are renovated" to "were renovated"

2. "was featured" to "is featured"

3. "was located" to "is located"

PAGE 80

Writing Tip 1

Nobody had lived in that house for fifteen years.

PAGE 82

Writing Tip 2

(Answers will vary. Here are two options.)

There are 45,000 deaths from car accidents yearly in the USA.

Car accidents cause 45,000 deaths yearly in the USA.

Grammar Clinic

Capitalization (Exercises for Practice)

(Changes to be made by the student are underlined *and set in* **boldface** *type.)*

1. The **p**eople of **N**ew **O**rleans, Louisiana, celebrate the Mardi Gras **f**estival in **F**ebruary.
2. **T**he main religions in **J**apan are Buddhism, **S**hintoism, and Christianity.
3. Last **m**onth, **I** saw **R**oman **H**oliday, a movie starring Audrey Hepburn, on **t**elevision.
4. If **y**ou visit **S**an Francisco, **y**ou should be sure to see the **G**olden **G**ate **B**ridge.
5. **B**oston **U**niversity is just a short distance from **L**ogan **I**nternational **A**irport.
6. On our trip to **C**anada, we went to Niagara Falls, **L**ake **L**ouise, **a**nd the **V**ictoria **M**useum.
7. **M**arco's **f**ather, Tomas, is from a small town just **n**orth of Mexico City.
8. **C**an you believe it? Joe speaks **F**rench, **I**talian, **S**panish, and **K**orean!
9. In **N**ew **Z**ealand, **s**ummer comes in **J**anuary, and **w**inter is in July.
10. She loves to study many **s**ubjects, but **B**usiness **E**nglish 101 and poetry are her favorites.

Punctuation (Exercises for Practice)

(End-of-sentence punctuation shown here should have been added by students.)

1. There is a holiday next Friday.
2. Who is your favorite singer?
3. Is there a police station nearby?
4. I really love strawberry ice cream!
5. Have you ever eaten chocolate pizza?
6. Her mother lives in Florida.
7. That's fantastic!
8. Where did you go last summer?
9. I bought a car on Sunday.
10. Summers in Hong Kong are too hot!

(Sentence 9 could end with an exclamation point instead of a period and Sentences 4 and 10 could end with a period instead of an exclamation point; either punctuation is correct.)

Listing Adjectives (Exercises for Practice)

1. Last Saturday, Ann bought an expensive brown leather jacket.
2. After the movie, we ate some rich, delicious chocolate cake.
3. George lives in a big, old, white house that is not too far from Philadelphia.
4. Mark is looking for a beautiful tall, young woman to marry.
5. In the corner, there is a hundred-year-old, brown oak rocking chair.
6. The lovers met in a quiet little French restaurant.

(The rule is not perfect, and Sentence 4 could also read, "Mark is looking for a tall, beautiful, young woman to marry.")

PAGE 104

Simple Sentences (Exercises for Practice)

(Accept equivalent questions.)

1. My brother, in a fast moving car. *fragment (What is he doing?)*
   (S over "brother")

2. Many of the students in this class are women.
   (S over "Many", V over "are")

3. Kevin Costner is excellent in his new film.
   (S over "Kevin", V over "is")

4. After we won the game, everyone went to a big party.
   (S over "everyone", V over "went")

5. In Jim's big, empty room, a calendar and mirror still on the wall. *fragment (What are they doing there?)*
   (S1 over "calendar", S2 over "mirror")

6. All of the club members are going to the party.
   (S over "All", V over "are going")

7. Before 1960, very few families had televisions.
   (S over "families", V over "had")

8. Playing tennis every night until midnight, in the light of the moon. *fragment (Who is playing?)*
   (V over "Playing")

9. In the southern part of Florida sports cars are very popular.
   (S over "cars", V over "are")

10. Some of the new English rock groups have a great sound.
    (S over "Some", V over "have")

11. Many sumo wrestlers weigh over 400 pounds.
    (S over "wrestlers", V over "weigh")

12. Usually eat pizza and go dancing on Saturday nights. *fragment (Who eats and goes dancing?)*
    (V over "eat", V over "go")

PAGE 106

Simple Sentence Patterns (Exercises for Practice)

1. We went (to Washington, D.C.), last spring and had a great time.
   (S V1 over "We went", V2 over "had")

2. The manager (of the baseball team) is talking (to the pitcher).
   (S over "manager", V over "is talking")

3. (Under the stack of books), my homework is waiting (for me).
   (S over "homework", V over "is waiting")

4. (After the end of the movie), the people came (out of the theater) slowly.
   (S over "people", V over "came")

5. Central Station is (at the end) (of Main Street).
   (S over "Station", V over "is")

6. Last night I stayed up very late and watched an old movie (on TV).
   (S V1 over "I stayed", V2 over "watched")

7. (After the graduation ceremony), we are going (to the party) (at the Plaza Hotel).
   (S over "we", V over "are going")

8. The dog and cat came (into the kitchen) and ate all the cookies (on Sunday).
   (S1 over "dog", S2 V1 over "cat came", V2 over "ate")

9. Last year I took Business English 101.
   (S over "I", V over "took")

10. (On Sundays), Kathy goes (to the gym), practices aerobics, and takes a sauna.
    (S V1 over "Kathy goes", V2 over "practices", V3 over "takes")

PAGE 108

Compound Sentences (Exercises for Practice)

(Students should have circled words shown in parentheses in this Answer Key.)

1. <u>C</u> Lisa saw a strange man following her, (so) she went to the nearest police station.
   (S V over "Lisa saw", S V over "she went")

2. <u>S</u> Before the game, we all stopped at a pizza parlor for lunch.

3. <u>C</u> Punk music was popular in the 1980s, (but) it wasn't popular (for long).

4. <u>C</u> Jean-Luc won first prize in the ski competition, (so) his hometown had a big celebration.

5. <u>S</u> The thief jumped onto a moving train, climbed inside, and hid in a sleeping compartment.

6. <u>C</u> A young boy was sleeping in the back of the class, (but) the teacher didn't notice.

Sentence Writing

(Answers may vary. These are likely.)

1. Jim went skiing, and he had a wonderful time.

2. The car broke down, so we couldn't go camping.

3. Mary is in love with Bill, but she doesn't want to marry him.

PAGE 110

Complex Sentences (Exercises for Practice)

(First Group)

1. <u>(Before) he met Juliet, Romeo didn't know the meaning of love.</u>

2. <u>Yuri studies English (because) he wants to work in Seattle.</u>

3. <u>Wei-Ming saw all her old friends (while) she was home.</u>

4. <u>(If) you believe in yourself, you can move mountains.</u>

(Second Group)

1. Sally came in quietly after the class started.

    After the class started, Sally came in quietly.

2. Juan listened to the radio while he cooked dinner.

    While he cooked dinner, Juan listened to the radio.

PAGE 112

Using Articles (Exercises for Practice)

(Accept reasonable alternate answers.)

Last week, I bought __a__ new Walkman. Since I wanted to get __a__ good price, I went to __the__ biggest discount store in town. I looked at __many__ personal stereos and asked __a lot of__ questions before I made my choice. At first, __the__ personal stereos all seemed good. Then I found __a__ very small one selling for half price, so I bought it. I use it for studying English and for listening to music on my way to school. I also have __some__ money left over because it was so inexpensive. I'm going to use __the__ money I saved to buy some rock and roll tapes to listen to on my way to school.

PAGE 114

Subject–Verb Agreement (Exercises for Practice)

(Changed words are **boldfaced** *and* underlined.*)*

1. Electronics **is** very important to Japanese economic success.
2. Neither of the boys **plays** the piano like their father.
3. OK
4. The first-year students or the second-year students **take** Saturday off.
5. The radio news **is** good for listening practice.
6. The car behind all those oak trees **is** ten years old.
7. OK
8. Many young people, like my brother Willy, **enjoy** eating ethnic food.
9. This school, with almost four thousand students, **uses** a lot of paper every day.
10. Last night many people **were** at the concert.

PAGE 116

Verb Tense Consistency (Exercises for Practice)

(Changed verbs are **boldfaced** *and* underlined.)

1. Sally **ate** pizza, and Anna ate tuna salad.

   OR Sally eats pizza, and Anna **eats** tuna salad.
2. When you mix red and yellow paint, you **get** orange.

   OR When you **mixed** red and yellow paint, you got orange.
3. Last year Sung **tried** to do his best.
4. Tom caught the football and **ran** to the goal line.

   OR Tom **catches** the football and runs to the goal line.
5. Marie knew that it **would be** a romantic evening with Bill.

   OR Marie **knows** that it will be a romantic evening with Bill.
6. Last weekend, I **went** to the movies with some friends.
7. At first, Larry hated to eat sushi, but later he **started** to **like** it.
8. Regular exercise is good for your health and **helps** you lose weight.

   OR Regular exercise is good for your health and **will help** you lose weight.
9. When parents divorce, it **causes** problems for the children.
10. In dance clubs, disco music is not very popular these days; most people **prefer** techno, rap, and hip hop.

PAGE 118

Pronoun Agreement (Exercises for Practice)

(Changed words are **boldfaced** *and* underlined.*)*

1. Many pop songs have romance as **their** topic.
2. After she washed the shirts with bleach, **they were** as white as snow.
3. My teacher and his wife are planning to buy **their** own home.
4. Mary went to aerobics class three times a week so **she** could lose weight.
5. A student asked the teacher to explain **his** grades.

   OR A student asked the teacher to explain **her** grades.

6. European cities are famous around the world for **their** architecture, art, and food.

7. Yung-Hee hung up her raincoat on the balcony and let **it** dry all day.

8. Most students know **they** can't learn English without work.

9. Some guy tried to get my phone number, but **he was** unsuccessful.

10. The twin sisters are famous, because **they are** one hundred years old.

(Sentence 8 can also be called correct as printed in the Student Book if the "you" is considered to be a generic "you" with the meaning of "one.")

PAGE 120

Use of Commas (Exercises for Practice)

(Students should have added commas as shown here.)

1. Richard likes to play tennis, baseball, golf, and rugby.

2. One beautiful Saturday afternoon, we went downtown and saw a movie.

3. New York, Paris, and Milan are important fashion centers.

4. When the big earthquake started, we ran outside.

5. Until Akiko graduated, she worked at a bookstore.

6. Sydney, an exciting city, is going to host many foreign visitors for the Olympics.

7. Romance, youth, and money are difficult to keep.

8. Last night we went out to dinner, but we came home early

    OR Last night, we went out to dinner, but we came home early.

9. The pizza had shrimp, mushrooms, corn, tuna, and chocolate.

10. We will meet at Central Park, have a picnic, and watch the fireworks.

Words in Motion— Reproducible Resources

The materials on the following pages may be duplicated for classroom use. A convenient way of using them is to make as many copies of each as you believe you will use during the term and keep them in folders, ready to distribute when they are needed. The reproducible resources include those listed below. (Note that the Learning Logs for Parts 1 and 2 are also found on pages 26 and 55 of the Student Book and the Correction Symbols appear on the inside back cover of the Student Book as well as in this Guide.)

Correction Symbols

Symbol	Kind of Error	Example
C	capitalization	My birthday is in january. (C above january)
P	punctuation	It's a great movie? (P above ?)
¶	new paragraph	¶ (start a new paragraph)
sp	spelling	We luve chocolate. (sp above luve)
WF	word form	He is a gently person. (WF above gently)
pl/sg	plural/singular mistake	I have three sister. (pl/sg above sister)
s/v	subject-verb agreement	She like swimming. (s/v above like)
VT	verb tense mistake	Last week we have a great party. (VT above have)
∅	delete (erase)	I'm going to shopping tonight.
∧	add something	It is beautiful afternoon. (a above ∧)
ww	wrong word	Turn write at the corner. (ww above write)
#	count/non-count mistake	How many money did you bring? (# above many)
conj.	conjunction mistake	And we studied drama. (conj. above And)
∿	reverse word order	That is a very book long.
wo	word order mistake	I you see will later. (wo above)
/	separate these words	Class is over at three.
‿	should be one word	Every body is late today.
RW	rewrite (meaning unclear)	I used to every often. (RW above)

Writer's Checklist _____

Project _____ Date Due _____

**Use this checklist to review your finished composition before you give it to your teacher.
Check (✓) each item as you answer it.**

_____ **1.** Did you double-space (leave a space between lines)?

_____ **2.** Did you write your name at the top of the paper?

_____ **3.** Did you write the date at the top of the paper?

_____ **4.** Did you give a title to your composition? If it is a letter, did you write a greeting, closing, and signature?

_____ **5.** Did you capitalize the start of each sentence?

_____ **6.** Did you use the correct punctuation at the end of each sentence?

_____ **7.** Did you indent the start of each paragraph?

_____ **8.** Did you use new paragraphs to show new topics or ideas?

_____ **9.** Did you begin with an interesting opening?

_____ **10.** Did you end with a conclusion that adds a final thought or idea?

_____ **11.** Did you spell every word correctly?

_____ **12.** Did you check your writing to see if you avoided the kinds of mistakes you made before?

Mistake Log

One way to help make sure you don't repeat the same kind of mistakes over and over is to keep track of them in a log. Use this page to keep a record of your writing mistakes.

List the kinds of mistakes you make. If you repeat the same mistake on another writing assignment, then add a check (✓) in the "Repeated" column for that kind of mistake. When you finish your next writing assignment, review your work for the kinds of mistakes you made before.

Date	Kind of Mistake	Example	Repeated

Learning Log for Part 1_____

1. **Think back:** Read the short review of Part 1 below. Circle the activities or topics you enjoyed the most. Underline the skills you want more help with.

   In Part 1, you practiced various skills for developing ideas, writing, editing, and revising. These included note-taking, writing from notes, making lists, Quick Writes, peer editing, revision marking, and rewriting. You had a chance to write about your home and family, personal interests and hobbies, and dreams for the future.

2. **Look back:** Look through the pages of Part 1 to remember the activities and see your work again.

3. **Write about it:** Answer these questions to tell your teacher more about your progress.

   1. What were your favorite activities in Part 1 of this book?

   _____

   _____

   _____

   _____

   2. What do you want more help with?

   _____

   _____

   _____

   _____

Vocabulary Notes

Now look back over your work and writings in Units 1 through 5 and find vocabulary words you want to remember. Write them on the lines below.

_____

_____

_____

_____

_____

Learning Log for Part 2

1. **Think back:** Read the short review of Part 2 below. Circle the activities or topics you enjoyed the most. Underline the skills you want more help with.

   In Part 2, you practiced various skills for writing letters. You compared friendly and formal letters. You wrote a formal letter to request information. You looked at friendly letters and practiced describing a place and telling a story. Then you followed a "recipe" for a letter to keep in touch. To improve your letter, you used peer editing for interest and editing for form. Finally, you rewrote your letter.

2. **Look back:** Look through the pages of Part 2 to remember the activities and see your work again.

3. **Write about it:** Answer these questions to tell your teacher more about your progress.

   1. What were your favorite activities in Part 2 of this book?

   _____

   _____

   _____

   _____

   2. What do you want more help with?

   _____

   _____

   _____

   _____

Vocabulary Notes

Now look back over your work and writings in Units 6 through 10 and find vocabulary words you want to remember. Write them on the lines below.

_____

_____

_____

_____

_____

_____

General Learning Log

Like the learning logs at the ends of Part 1 and Part 2 of the book, this form will help you review your work, think about your progress, remember what you have learned, and focus on areas where you would like more work.

First look back over your work, including the pages in *Words in Motion,* your own notes, research, drafts, and any exercises to remember what you have done.

Kinds of Writing

1. What kind of writing have you been working on recently (for example, information letters, movie reviews)?

   _____

2. What is the purpose of this kind of writing? (See the Project Planning Form.) _____

   _____

3. Who are the readers you were writing for?_____

   _____

Skills Practiced

4. What language skills did you practice (include grammar points, useful phrases or sentences, and special vocabulary)?

   _____

   _____

5. What writing skills did you practice (include kinds of pre-writing or research, forms for organizing a kind of writing, and editing, revision, and rewriting skills)?

   _____

   _____

Thoughts and Feelings about Writing

6. What were the most enjoyable parts of this writing work?_____

   _____

   _____

7. What skills or activities are most useful for your needs? _____

   _____

8. What activities made you feel most successful?_____

_____

9. What skills or activities do you need to practice more?_____

_____

10. What advice would you give to other students starting this same writing work?_____

_____

Extra: Writer's Notebook

If you are keeping a Writer's Notebook, use the following checklist to help you.

_____ **1. Pre-writing**

Do you have all your pre-writing (including notes, lists, idea bubbles, Quick Writes, and any articles or other information gathered for research)?

_____ **2. Drafts**

Do you have all your drafts, revision markings and added ideas, sentences, and paragraphs?

_____ **3. Peer and Teacher Comments**

Do you have all your editing comments from classmates and suggestions and comments from your teacher?

_____ **4. Vocabulary**

Do you have all the vocabulary lists and practice sheets that go with the writing work you are now doing?

Keep all your work for your current writing work or project together in your notebook so you can find it easily. It is a good idea to add dividers to mark the sections of your notebook. Finally, you can put this Learning Log in the notebook as well after you show it to your teacher.

Vocabulary Study Tools_____

These vocabulary pages give you several "tools" or ways to study and remember new vocabulary. Try each way one time, and after that use one or more of the tools that seem most useful for the kinds of vocabulary you are working on.

Vocabulary Study Tool Number 1: Group Words by Meaning

1. One good way to study and remember vocabulary words is to group them by meaning. It is much easier to recall groups of similar words than a long list with no connection or theme. Look at this example:

List with no connection

violet	secretary	secretary	clever
salesman	brown	angry	joyous
industrious	brilliant	bright	banker
teacher	lazy	hard working	silly
silly	waitress	actor	gentle
lavender	gold	blue	intelligent

Organized or grouped by meaning

lazy industrious hard working		joyous silly angry gentle
teacher actor banker waitress salesman secretary	violet gold blue lavender brown	bright brilliant intelligent clever

2. Now list the new vocabulary you have learned. Then you will get a chance to group or organize them by meaning, just as the words above were organized.

_____ _____ _____

_____ _____ _____

_____ _____ _____

_____ _____ _____

_____ _____ _____

_____ _____ _____

3. Now group or organize some of the new words you wrote by meaning. There are many ways to group words, so find the one that seems natural to you. Write your groups of words on another piece of paper.

Vocabulary Study Tool Number 2: Group Words by Parts of Speech

1. Read the list of words below. They include different parts of speech.

student	to	pretty
for	teacher	and
well	brown	or
go	so	badly
family	learn	went
on	happy	quietly

2. Now look at the list below. The same words are organized by what part of speech each one is.

Noun	Verb	Adjective	Adverb	Preposition	Conjunction
student	go	pretty	well	to	and
teacher	learn	brown	badly	for	or
family	went	happy	quietly	on	so

3. Go back to your list of new words. List each one on the Vocabulary Practice Sheets on pages 68 and 69. Add the part of speech, a definition, and a sentence that uses the word.

Vocabulary Practice Sheets

EXAMPLE:

vocabulary	**part of speech**	**definition**
happy	*adjective*	*full of joy*

example sentence

I was happy to get your letter yesterday.

_____

vocabulary	**part of speech**	**definition**
_____	_____	_____

example sentence

_____

_____

vocabulary	**part of speech**	**definition**
_____	_____	_____

example sentence

_____

_____

vocabulary   **part of speech**   **definition**

_____   _____   _____

example sentence

_____

_____

vocabulary   **part of speech**   **definition**

_____   _____   _____

example sentence

_____

_____

vocabulary   **part of speech**   **definition**

_____   _____   _____

example sentence

_____

_____

vocabulary   **part of speech**   **definition**

_____   _____   _____

example sentence

_____

_____

vocabulary   **part of speech**   **definition**

_____   _____   _____

example sentence

_____

_____

Vocabulary Study Tool Number 3: Use Synonyms and Antonyms

1. Using the same word again and again makes your writing boring. Using a variety of words to talk about something makes your writing more interesting. Using synonyms and antonyms can help you. A synonym is a word that means the same as another word. An antonym is a word that means the opposite of a word. Look at the example of synonyms and antonyms of "interesting" below.

interesting

synonyms (same meaning)		antonyms (different meaning)	
entertaining	stimulating	dull	flat
fascinating	absorbing	tedious	tiresome
		boring	uninteresting

2. Next, try to put the following synonyms and antonyms of "helpful" below in their correct places in the chart. Place as many words as you can before you use your dictionary.

beneficial	worthless	constructive	useful
destructive	practical	harmful	useless

helpful

synonyms	antonyms
_____	_____
_____	_____
_____	_____
_____	_____

3. Now list words you have learned recently and other words that you think may help you to make your writing interesting. (Adjectives are best for this exercise.)

word	part of speech	definition

4. Pick four words from this list and write them in the chart below. Then use your memory, your dictionary, and, if you have one, a thesaurus to help you write synonyms and antonyms for each word.

1) _____

synonyms   **antonyms**

_____   _____

_____   _____

_____   _____

_____   _____

2) _____

synonyms   **antonyms**

_____   _____

_____   _____

_____   _____

_____   _____

3) _____

synonyms   **antonyms**

_____   _____

_____   _____

_____   _____

_____   _____

4) _____

synonyms   **antonyms**

_____   _____

_____   _____

_____   _____

_____   _____

Use these synonyms and antonyms to build your vocabulary and make your writing more interesting.